Life's Journey: A Guide to Effective Parenting and Healthy Relationships

OrangeBooks Publication

1st Floor, Rajhans Arcade, Mall Road, Kohka, Bhilai, Chhattisgarh 490020

Website:**www.orangebooks.in**

© Copyright, 2024, Author

All rights reserved. No part of this book may be reproduced, stored in a retrieval system, or transmitted, in any form by any means, electronic, mechanical, magnetic, optical, chemical, manual, photocopying, recording or otherwise, without the prior written consent of its writer.

First Edition, 2024
ISBN: 978-93-6554-573-9

Life's Journey

**A Guide to Effective Parenting and Healthy Relationships
(Stories, Activities, and Life lessons)**

VIKAS GUPTA

OrangeBooks Publication
www.orangebooks.in

Dedication

This book is born from the depths of my own journey through the involved web of relationships and the challenging path of staring from my childhood and to being a parent myself.

It is a reflection of the joys, pains, failures, the doubts that haunted my nights and triumphs that have shaped my understanding of what it means to nurture connections with those we love.

Each misstep has taught me lessons that have deepened my understanding of love, connection, and the importance of Nature that nurturing us.

These experiences were my greatest teachers, revealing the true essence of resilience, patience, and unconditional love.

To my parent & children, who have been my greatest inspiration and my most important responsibility—thank you for your patience as I learned to be the child & parent you deserved. And to all the families who strive to build healthy, loving relationships despite the inevitable challenges, may this book serve as a beacon of hope and guidance.

May we all continue to grow, heal, and cherish the connections that make our lives meaningful.

With gratitude for the Life's journey,

Vikas Gupta

Content

Life's Journey 1
- A Guide to Effective Parenting and Healthy Relationships 1

Relationship Excursion 2
- Explore, Experience & Realize Most Important Aspects of Life- "Relationship" 3
- Importance of Relationship at Various Stages of Life 7
  - ➤ The Journey of Life: A Tale of Relationships 8

Nurturing Relationships Through Nature: A Lifelong Journey 13
- Story: "Roots of Connection" A Journey Through the Banyan Tree" 14

Parenting Excursion 21
- Explore, Experience & Realize Most Important Aspects of Life- "Parenting with a Difference" 22
- Introduction: 24
- Challenges & Need 26
- Road Map for Parenting Excursion: 29
- Understanding Different Parenting Styles and Approaches 30
- Knowing, Understanding and Accepting The Child and Their Feelings 34
  - ➤ Story: "The Garden of Understanding" 34
- Building Trust, Confidence, Self-Esteem, And Decisiveness: 43
  - ➤ Story: "The Adventures of Akshaj and Araina" 43

- "Walk The Talk" Approach: 50
  - Story: " Walking Together: A Tale of Two Families" 50
- Gratitude Practice and Humbleness 57
  - Story: "Seeds of Gratitude" 57
- Importance of Health, Fitness & Nutrition 64
  - A Journey to Health and Happiness: An Indian Tale of Fitness and Nutrition 64
- Causes of Obesity in Children & Means to Control it 71
  - Story: The Green Revolution: Akshaj and Araina's Journey to Health 71
- Explaining Moral & Ethical Values and Dangers of Immoral Values 79
  - Story: "The Lesson of the Banyan Tree" 79
- Screen Time, Virtual and Technology Addition 86
  - Ishan's Adventure: Discovering Balance Between Screens & Nature 86
- Inculcating Value of Money 95
  - Story: "Vihan's Journey to Financial Wisdom" 95
- Overcoming Helicopter Parenting Style 105
  - Story: The Kite of Independence 105
- Understanding Gaslighting Parenting Approach 114
  - Story: "A Journey to Truth" 116
- Role of Spirituality in Healthy Parenting Style 124
  - Story: "A Journey of Spiritual Parenting in the Heart of India" 124
- Peer Pressure and Influences in Parenting 133
  - Story: Resisting Peer Pressure: Aesika's Journey 133

- Allow our Children to Fail: As Failure is One of Biggest Teacher in Life 140
  - ➢ The Tale of Ishan and His Adventures in Nature 140
- Parenting Excursion with Chanakya 147
  - ➢ Parenting with Chanakya: An Inspirational Story 147
- Keeping our Child Safe Online 161
  - ➢ Story: A Journey of Safe Surfing: Arya's Online Adventure 161
- Developing Socialization Skills in Children at Early Stage 170
  - ➢ Story: "A Journey to the Circle of Friends: Arjun's Story" 170
- Nurturing our Child's Potential 179
  - ➢ Story: The Seeds of Potential 179
- Nurturing Roots and Wings: Essance of Cultural Parenting 190
  - ➢ Story: Arjun's Journey: Nurturing Roots and Wings through Cultural Parenting 190

Early Life Enrichment Gateway: 198
- A Foundations for a Fulfilling Life 198
  - ➢ "The Journey of Rohan: Foundations for a Fulfilling Life" 198
- The Silent Teachers: Understanding the Role of Role Models in Parenting 205
  - ➢ Story: "The Seeds of Tomorrow" 205
- Emotionally Intelligent Parenting: Boost our Child's Emotional IQ 215
  - ➢ Emotional Intelligence: The Story of Aarav and His Family 217

- Emotional Intelligence (EI) Parenting Process Through Activities and Games 221
- Emotionally Safe Parenting: Valuing, Understanding, And Securing Children's Growth 225
    - Story: Beneath the Banyan: Nurturing Emotionally Safe Parenting 228
- Individuality vs. Obedience: Balancing Act for Crafting Well-Rounded Children in Today's Competitive Environment 235
    - Story: The Banyan Tree and the Kite: A Tale of Individuality and Obedience 236
- Building Bridges: Crossing Parent-Child Conflicts with Creative Solutions 245
    - Story: "Navigating the Tides of Change: An Inspirational Journey of a Parent-Child Relationship in India" 246
- AI / ChatGPT-Enhanced Parenting for Balanced Child Growth 257
    - Story: Nina's New Learning Companion 257

Adolescence Bliss Excursion 266

- Road Map for Adolescence Bliss Excursion: 268
- Challenges Faced by Today's Teenagers & Means to Overcoming it 269
    - Story: "Finding Balance in Nature: A Journey of Overcoming Teen Challenges" 269
- Adolescent Affiliation & Relationship Issues: Key Area of Realization 275
    - Story: The Journey to Heartfelt Connections 275
- Values for Teenagers 283
    - Story: "Nature's Classroom: Lessons of Life for Teenagers" 283

- Life Skills for Teenagers 292
  - Story: "The Journey of Growth: An Adventure in the Western Ghats" 292

"Loveventure Getaway" 300

- LoveVenture Getaway: An Inspirational Story 301
  - Story: "The Journey to Rekindle Love" 301
- "LoveVenture Getaway" 305
- Building Healthy Couples' Relationship 307

"Grand Generational Bond" 312

- The Tale of the Grand Generational Bond 313
- Road Map: "Grand Generational Bond" 318
  - Road Map: "Grand Generational Bond" 318
- **Early Adulthood Well-Being** 323
  - Early Adulthood Well-being: An Inspirational Story 323
- **Middle Adulthood Well-Being** 331
  - The Tale of Rekha: Embracing Middle Adulthood with Nature 331
- **Late Adulthood Well-Being** 341
  - Late Adulthood Well-being: An Inspirational Story 341

Life's Journey
A Guide To Effective Parenting And Healthy Relationships

(Stories, Activities, and Life lessons)

Relationship Excursion

Explore, Experience & Realize Most Important Aspects of Life- "Relationship"

Why?
Significance & role of "Relationship":

1. **Childhood:** Foundation for emotional development.

2. **Adolescence:** Shaping identity and social skills.

3. **Adulthood**: Support, companionship, and shared life.

4. **Elderly:** Vital for mental well-being, combating isolation.

What?
"Excursion"

1. **Childhood:**
- **Nature Exploration:** Introduce children to the wonders of the natural world through playful activities, fostering a sense of curiosity and connection with the environment.
- **Activities:** Nature walks, bird watching, and interactive games that encourage discovery and appreciation for the diversity of flora and fauna.

2. **Adolescence:**
- **Adventure and Learning:** Provide adventurous experiences that challenge and educate adolescents, promoting teamwork, resilience, and a deeper understanding of ecological systems.
- **Activities:** Hiking, camping, and environmental workshops that combine physical activity with hands-on learning about ecosystems and conservation.

3. **Adulthood:**
- **Wellness and Relaxation:** Focus on nature excursions that offer adults an opportunity to unwind, recharge, and find solace in natural surroundings, promoting mental and physical well-being.
- **Activities:** Yoga retreats, mindfulness hikes, and nature-based spa experiences that emphasize relaxation and connection with the natural world.

4. **Elderly Years:**
- **Therapeutic Nature Retreats:** Tailor excursions to cater to the needs of the elderly, providing gentle activities that enhance their overall well-being and allow for reflection.
- **Activities:** Visting holy place, lake-side, river side camping and meditation, mountain, beach, Jungle, Botanical Garden visits, scenic drives, and gentle nature walks, offering a serene and tranquil setting for relaxation and reminiscence.

How?

"Relationship Excursion"

Nature and activity-based Relationship excursion" is an approach that emphasizes engaging person in outdoor activities, exploring nature, and incorporating hands-on experiences into their learning and development.

This type of excursion involves taking person outside of their usual environment to participate in activities that foster a connection with nature and promote physical, cognitive, and social development.

Trips to nature reserves, or other outdoor spaces where they can explore, play, and learn from their surroundings.

The activities planned during these excursions are often designed to be interactive, allowing them to engage with the natural world and develop various skills while having fun.

Take Ways ?

Nature and activity-based excursions contribute to overall well-being at various stages of life by providing:

1. **Childhood:**
- **Physical Development:** Outdoor activities enhance motor skills and physical fitness.
- **Intellectual Growth:** Exploration in nature stimulates curiosity and intellectual development.
- **Emotional Well-being**: Exposure to natural environments promotes emotional resilience and reduces stress.

2. **Adolescence:**
- **Social development:** Encourages teamwork and communication skills.
- **Stress reduction:** Acts as a healthy outlet for academic and social pressures.
- **Self-Discovery:** Nature excursions aid in identity formation and self-awareness.
- **Physical fitness:** Supports a healthy lifestyle and habits.

3. **Adulthood:**
- **Stress relief:** Offers a break from routine, reducing work-related stress.
- **Relationship building:** Provides opportunities for bonding with family and friends.
- **Physical health:** Supports cardiovascular health through outdoor activities.
- **Connection:** Nature provides opportunities for social bonding and community engagement.

4. **Elderly years:**
- **Mental well-being:** Combats feelings of isolation and depression.
- **Emotional Well-being:** Connecting with nature fosters a sense of purpose and fulfillment.
- **Social Connection:** Group excursions foster a sense of community and reduce isolation.
- **Physical Activity:** Contributes to maintaining mobility and flexibility.
- **Quality of Life:** Enhances overall life satisfaction and a sense of purpose.

In all stages, nature and activity-based excursions have a holistic impact on physical, mental, and emotional well-being

Importance of Relationship at Various Stages of Life

The Journey of Life: A Tale of Relationships

Early Childhood (Infancy to 5 years)

In a small village in India, a little girl named Araina was born into a loving family. Her parents, Vikas and Vidhi, showered her with affection and provided a nurturing environment. Araina's early years were filled with warmth and security, which helped her develop a strong attachment to her parents. This bond gave her the confidence to explore her surroundings and learn new things.

In contrast, Araina's cousin, Aditya, who lived nearby, didn't receive the same level of attention. His parents were often busy with work and didn't have much time for him. As a result, Aditya struggled with anxiety and had difficulty forming bonds with others.

Childhood (6 to 12 years)

As Araina grew older, she formed close friendships with her classmates. She was particularly close to her best friend, Priya. Together, they navigated the challenges of school and peer pressure. Araina's parents continued to play a crucial role, guiding her through the ups and downs of childhood and teaching her the values of honesty and kindness.

Aditya, on the other hand, found it hard to make friends. Without a strong support system at home, he often felt isolated and succumbed to peer pressure, leading to poor decisions and conflicts at school.

Adolescence (13 to 18 years)

During her teenage years, Araina experienced the typical struggles of adolescence. She had her first crush, faced academic pressures, and sometimes clashed with her parents. However, the open communication and trust she had with her parents helped her navigate these challenges. Her parents respected her growing need for independence while providing the guidance she needed. Aditya's teenage years were turbulent. The lack of a supportive family environment and meaningful friendships led to an identity crisis. He rebelled against authority and made choices that negatively impacted his future.

Early Adulthood (19 to 40 years)

Araina went to college, where she met many new people and formed lifelong friendships. She also fell in love with Karan, whom she later married. Their relationship was built on mutual respect, love, and shared goals. Araina's strong foundation from her childhood helped her balance her career and personal life effectively.

Aditya, lacking a supportive network, struggled to find his footing. His relationships were often strained, and he faced difficulties in both his personal and professional life. The absence of strong bonds made him feel disconnected and lonely.

Middle Adulthood (41 to 60 years)

In her middle adulthood, Araina juggled various responsibilities, including raising her children and advancing in her career. She maintained close ties with her parents, siblings, and friends. These relationships provided her with a robust support system, helping her navigate the challenges of this life stage.

Aditya's middle years were marked by a midlife crisis. The lack of close relationships made it hard for him to cope with the stressors of life. He felt overwhelmed and struggled to find meaning and purpose.

Late Adulthood (61 years and beyond)

As Araina entered her senior years, she enjoyed the fruits of a life filled with meaningful relationships. Her children visited her regularly, and she remained active in her community. Her social connections kept her mentally and emotionally healthy.

Aditya, now in his late adulthood, faced isolation. With few close relationships and little social support, he struggled with loneliness and depression. The absence of a supportive network took a toll on his mental and physical health.

Key Takeaways: Araina's story demonstrates the power of strong, healthy relationships at every stage of life. Her secure early childhood laid the foundation for a lifetime of positive connections and emotional well-being. In contrast, Aditya's lack of supportive relationships led to numerous struggles, highlighting the negative impacts of isolation and poor social bonds.

Strategies for Building and Maintaining Healthy Relationships:

1. **Effective Communication:** Always keep the lines of communication open. Listen actively and speak honestly.

2. **Empathy:** Try to understand others' perspectives and feelings.

3. **Support:** Be there for your loved ones in times of need.

4. **Boundaries:** Respect each other's boundaries to maintain healthy dynamics.

5. **Quality Time:** Spend quality time with family and friends to strengthen bonds.

By fostering strong relationships, we can navigate the challenges of life more effectively and enjoy a richer, more fulfilling existence.

Importance of Relationship at various stages of Life

Relationships play a crucial role at various stages of life, contributing significantly to personal development, emotional well-being, and overall life satisfaction. The importance of relationships evolves over time, and each stage brings unique challenges. Here's a brief overview of the importance of relationships at different stages of life, the challenges they may present, and strategies to overcome them:

1. **Early Childhood (Infancy to 5 years):**
- **Importance:** Early relationships with caregivers lay the foundation for emotional and social development. They provide a sense of security and help in forming attachment bonds critical for future relationships.
- **Challenges:** Limited communication skills may lead to frustration. Balancing independence and dependence are a challenge.

- **Overcoming Challenges**: Foster a secure attachment by responding to the child's needs. Encourage exploration while providing a secure base.

2. **Childhood (6 to 12 years):**
- **Importance:** Friendships become more influential. Family & teacher relationships continue to shape values and social skills.
- **Challenges:** Peer pressure and developing a sense of identity may create conflicts.
- **Overcoming Challenges:** Encourage open communication. Teach problem-solving and decision-making skills. Provide guidance on choosing positive friendships.

3. **Adolescence (13 to 18 years):**
- **Importance:** Relationships become more complex. Peer relationships, romantic interests, and family dynamics play pivotal roles in identity formation.
- **Challenges:** Struggles with independence, identity crisis, and peer influence can lead to conflicts.
- **Overcoming Challenges:** Foster open communication, respect autonomy, and provide guidance. Encourage healthy friendships and relationships.

4. **Early Adulthood (19 to 40 years):**
- **Importance:** Building intimate relationships becomes a focus. Friendships, family, and romantic relationships contribute to emotional support and personal growth.
- **Friendships and Professional Networks:** Building a social support system extends beyond family, with friendships and professional networks becoming key.
- **Challenges:** Balancing career, personal goals, and relationships. Navigating the transition to more mature, committed relationships.

- **Overcoming Challenges:** Prioritize communication and shared goals. Establish healthy boundaries. Invest time and effort in maintaining relationships.

5. **Middle Adulthood (41 to 60 years):**
- **Family and Work-Life Balance:** Nurturing relationships with a partner and children is essential, as is maintaining connections with friends and colleagues.
- **Parent-Adult Child Relationships:** Parents may experience evolving relationships with adult children, providing guidance and support as needed.
- **Challenges:** Juggling multiple responsibilities, potential midlife crises, and changes in family dynamics.
- **Overcoming Challenges:** Prioritize time for relationships. Adapt to changes together. Seek support when needed.

6. **Late Adulthood (61 years and beyond):**
- **Importance:** Social connections become crucial for mental health. Family relationships offer support and companionship.
- **Challenges:** Coping with loss, physical health decline, and potential isolation.
- **Overcoming Challenges:** Stay socially active. Seek support from family and friends. Engage in community activities. Embrace changing dynamics with resilience.

In general, effective communication, empathy, and adaptability are key skills to navigate relationship challenges at any stage of life. Building and maintaining strong relationships require effort, understanding, and a commitment to mutual growth and support.

In summary, relationships play a pivotal role in each stage of life, providing support, companionship, and opportunities for personal and social development. Cultivating and maintaining healthy relationships contributes significantly to overall well-being.

Nurturing Relationships Through Nature: A Lifelong Journey

Story: "Roots of Connection" A Journey Through the Banyan Tree"

Childhood - The Magic Garden

In a small village in Kerala, a young boy named Akshaj grew up surrounded by lush green fields and dense forests. His grandfather, an avid gardener, had a beautiful garden filled with vibrant flowers, fruit trees, and a majestic banyan tree that stood at the centre. Every evening, Akshaj would follow his grandfather into the garden, helping him water the plants and listen to stories about the birds and animals that visited.

Akshaj's sensory development thrived in this natural setting. He would feel the rough bark of the trees, smell the fragrant flowers, and hear the chirping of the birds. These experiences not only stimulated his senses but also fostered his cognitive and emotional growth. The time spent in the garden created a strong bond between Akshaj and his grandfather, building a foundation of trust and security.

However, Akshaj's friend, Raju, lived in a nearby town with little access to nature. His days were spent indoors, surrounded by screens and concrete. Raju often felt restless and struggled with anxiety, missing out on the emotional regulation that nature provided Akshaj.

Adolescence - The Sacred Grove

As Akshaj entered his teenage years, the banyan tree became his refuge. During times of academic stress and peer pressure, he would climb its sturdy branches and find solace in its shade. The tree offered him a space for solitude, where he could reflect on his identity and dreams. It was also a place where he and his friends would gather, sharing stories and strengthening their bonds.

Akshaj participated in environmental conservation projects initiated by his school, which nurtured his sense of responsibility towards nature. These activities not only fostered a sense of independence but also helped him build lasting friendships based on shared values.

Meanwhile, Raju's adolescence was marked by constant stress. The lack of a natural escape made it difficult for him to cope with academic pressures. His social interactions were limited to online platforms, leading to feelings of isolation and disconnection.

Adulthood - The Community Garden

As Akshaj grew older, he moved to the bustling city of Mumbai for work. The transition was overwhelming, but he found comfort in the city's community garden. He joined a group of nature enthusiasts who met regularly to tend to the plants. This shared activity helped him forge new friendships and strengthened his sense of community.

Regular exposure to nature mitigated Akshaj's stress and improved his mental health. He found joy in simple activities like cycling in the park or gardening, which kept him physically active and reduced the risk of chronic diseases. Engaging in outdoor activities with his wife and children created lasting memories and traditions, imparting values of environmental stewardship to the next generation.

In contrast, Raju's adult life was a constant struggle with stress and health issues. His sedentary lifestyle and lack of connection with nature took a toll on his physical and mental well-being. His relationships suffered as he found it challenging to balance work and family life without the restorative power of nature.

Midlife and Older Adulthood - The Banyan Tree's Legacy

Years later, Akshaj returned to his village with his family. The banyan tree, now even more majestic, stood as a symbol of continuity and purpose. It offered a space for reflection and a sense of peace during his midlife transition. Akshaj engaged in activities like bird watching and nature walks, which supported his cognitive health and kept him mentally sharp.

The community garden back in Mumbai continued to thrive, bringing together people from diverse backgrounds. These connections reduced feelings of loneliness and isolation among older adults, fostering a sense of belonging and shared purpose.

Meanwhile, Raju, who had neglected his connection with nature throughout his life, faced the challenges of aging with a sense of regret. The absence of a natural space for reflection made it difficult for him to find meaning and comfort in his later years.

End of Life - A Legacy of Love and Conservation

In his twilight years, Akshaj dedicated himself to conserving the natural spaces that had enriched his life. He planted trees, organized environmental awareness programs, and inspired future generations to cherish and protect nature. The banyan tree, under which he had experienced so much, stood as a testament to his legacy.

At the end of his life, Akshaj found spiritual comfort in nature. The interconnectedness he felt with the larger web of life provided solace, reinforcing the importance of nurturing relationships through nature.

Raju, on the other hand, faced the end of his life with a sense of disconnection. The absence of a lifelong relationship with nature left him without the spiritual and emotional support that Akshaj found so comforting.

Epilogue: The Lifelong Journey

Akshaj's story illustrates the profound impact nature can have on nurturing relationships and enhancing well-being throughout life. From childhood to old age, his connection with nature provided emotional regulation, stress relief, physical health, and social bonds. The flip side of Raju's story highlights the negative consequences of a life disconnected from nature.

Incorporating nature into our lives enriches our relationships and promotes a sustainable lifestyle. Nature's therapeutic and healing properties, coupled with its ability to build community connections, enhance empathy, and provide perspective, underscore its importance in nurturing healthy, resilient, and meaningful relationships throughout a person's life. By embracing nature, we not only enrich our own lives but also contribute to a legacy of conservation and respect for the natural world.

Nurturing Relationships Through Nature: A Lifelong Journey

The relationship between nature and the various life stages of a person is profound and can significantly impact their development, well-being, and relationships throughout their life cycle. Here's a breakdown of the importance of nature at different stages:

Childhood

- **Developmental Growth:** Interaction with nature stimulates all the senses and supports cognitive, physical, and emotional development in children. Outdoor play encourages creativity, problem-solving, and motor skills.

- **Foundation for Healthy Habits:** Early experiences with nature can instill a lifelong appreciation for the outdoors and promote activities that lead to a healthier lifestyle.

- **Emotional Regulation:** Nature has calming effects on children, reducing stress and fostering a sense of peace and well-being.

- **Sensory Development:** Engaging with nature helps in the sensory development of young children. Experiences like playing in the dirt, listening to birds, and smelling flowers stimulate their senses and can lead to more effective learning and development.

- **Bonding:** Shared experiences in nature, such as family walks or picnics, can strengthen bonds between children and their caregivers, creating lasting memories and a foundation of trust and security.\

Adolescence

- **Identity and Autonomy:** Nature can provide a backdrop for adolescents to explore their identity and independence, offering both solitude and a space for social interaction.

- **Stress Relief:** The teen years can be tumultuous, and nature serves as a respite from academic and social pressures, reducing anxiety and depression.

- **Environmental Stewardship:** Engaging with nature can cultivate a sense of responsibility and care for the environment, which can influence career choices and personal values.

- **Independence and Social Connections:** Outdoor activities like hiking, camping, or environmental conservation projects can foster a sense of independence in adolescents. They also provide opportunities for socializing and building new friendships based on shared interests.

Adulthood

- **Social Connections:** Shared experiences in nature, such as hiking, gardening, or community cleanup efforts, can strengthen relationships and foster new ones.
- **Mental Health:** Regular exposure to nature helps mitigate stress, enhances mood, and improves overall mental health, which is crucial for balancing the demands of work, family, and personal life.
- **Physical Health:** Active engagement with nature through activities like walking, cycling, or gardening promotes physical health and can reduce the risk of chronic diseases.
- **Parenting and Family Bonds:** Engaging in outdoor activities as a family can strengthen familial bonds, create lasting memories, and establish traditions. It offers a space for parents to teach children about the world around them, imparting values of environmental stewardship and respect for all living things.

Midlife and Older Adulthood

- **Life Reflection and Meaning:** Nature offers a space for reflection and can provide a sense of continuity and purpose, especially during life transitions such as retirement.
- **Cognitive Function:** Interaction with nature has been shown to support cognitive health in older adults, potentially delaying the onset of dementia and other cognitive impairments.
- **Social Engagement:** Activities connected with nature can help older adults remain engaged with their community, reducing feelings of loneliness and isolation.

End of Life

- **Legacy and Conservation:** A lifetime of experiences in nature can inspire a desire to conserve natural spaces for future generations, leading to actions that create a lasting legacy.

- **Spiritual Connection:** Nature can offer profound spiritual comfort and a sense of interconnectedness with the larger web of life, which can be particularly comforting at this life stage.

Throughout Life

1. **Therapeutic and Healing Properties:** Nature has inherent therapeutic qualities that can aid in healing and emotional support during challenging times. Shared experiences in natural settings can provide comfort and solace, helping to build or rebuild relationships through shared healing and mutual support.

2. **Building Community Connections:** Community gardens, conservation efforts, and outdoor group activities can bring together individuals from diverse backgrounds, fostering a sense of community and shared purpose. These activities encourage collaboration, mutual respect, and a sense of belonging, which are fundamental to building strong relationships.

3. **Enhancing Emotional Intelligence and Empathy:** Nature teaches empathy and sensitivity to the environment and to one another. By experiencing the interconnectedness of life, individuals may develop a deeper understanding and empathy towards others, enhancing their relationships.

4. **Reflection and Perspective:** Nature provides a space for reflection, allowing individuals to gain perspective on life's challenges. This reflective practice can lead to healthier relationship dynamics, as individuals are better equipped to deal with interpersonal issues calmly and constructively.

5. **Promoting Mindfulness and Presence**: Being in nature encourages mindfulness and being present in the moment, qualities that can

greatly enhance personal interactions. By being more present with others, individuals can forge deeper and more meaningful connections.

Incorporating nature into the fabric of our relationships not only enriches these connections but also promotes a sustainable lifestyle that respects and preserves the natural world for future generations. The intrinsic value of nature, combined with its myriad benefits for physical and mental well-being, underscores its importance in nurturing healthy, resilient, and meaningful relationships throughout a person's life.

Life's Journey: A Guide to Effective Parenting and Healthy Relationships

Parenting Excursion

Explore, Experience & Realize Most Important Aspects of Life- "Parenting with a Difference"

Why?

Significance of Parenting:

Nurture foundation for a child's physical, emotional, and cognitive development, shaping their future well-being and societal contribution and nation building.

What?

"Parenting Excursion"

An outing or activity in the lap of nature that involves parents and their children, where parenting skills or interactions play a central role. In a more general sense, it refers to any excursion or outing specifically designed for parents and their children to spend quality time together, engage in activities, and foster positive parent-child relationships.

How?

Nature and activity-based parenting excursion" is a parenting approach that emphasizes engaging children & parents in outdoor activities, exploring nature, and incorporating hands-on experiences into their learning and development.

This type of excursion involves taking parents & children outside of their usual environment to participate in activities that foster a connection with nature and promote physical, cognitive, and social development.

Trips to nature reserves, or other outdoor spaces where parents & children can explore, play, and learn from their surroundings.

The activities planned during these excursions are often designed to be interactive, allowing Parents & children to engage with the natural world and develop various skills while having fun.

This parenting style aims to provide a holistic learning experience, incorporating elements of environmental education, physical activity, and social interaction to support a child's overall growth and well-being

Introduction:

1. **"Parenting Excursion" is a process & place to share the doubts, learn all about "Raising the new age kids".**

Challenges in Raising the new age kids

- Friction |differences |disagreement | non-listener

- Low Confidence

- Lack of trust

- indecisiveness

- Virtual world – ever increasing screen time

- to scold or not? how to do so?

- Meeting their demand or not?

- eating and sleeping habits

There many queries in parents mind, but they lack proper guidance. To take care of these queues, to guide the parents to meet the challenges of "New age Parenting" we at LiveAdve are starting series of workshop for parents along with their kids.

Raising children in technologically advanced environment is not an easy task for new parents. It is easy to give mobile or tabs in child's hand but it is difficult to tell stories or give nutritious foods

Parent need to spend quality time with their children, which will balance their professional and personal goals. Warm, affectionate and aware parent can raise child into emotionally strong, mentally healthy & bright child.

We strive to make Parenting easier and more enjoyable via activity-based counselling, in the lap of nature, through our Professionals design activities, keeping all psychological and scientific factors in mind.

"Parenting Excursion" - aims to reach out parents to enrich them about their role's responsibility in their child's life.

Let us come together, to give children, the best childhood experience, a strong foundation to develop them into healthy & responsible adult.

Challenges & Need

Challenges & Need

The parenting landscape for the current generation is marked by a variety of challenges that both parents and children face. These challenges arise from changes in societal norms, technological advancements, economic pressures, and evolving family structures. Here are some key challenges faced by current generation parents and kids in the parenting process:

1. **Technology and Screen Time:** The pervasive use of technology and electronic devices can pose challenges for parents in managing screen time and ensuring that children engage in healthy and balanced activities.

2. **Social Media Influence:** Children and teenagers are often exposed to the pressures and challenges of social media, including cyberbullying, unrealistic body image standards, and the constant need for validation.

3. **Busy Lifestyles:** Many parents today juggle demanding work schedules, which can lead to time constraints for quality family interactions and involvement in children's activities.

4. **Helicopter Parenting:** Some parents may struggle to find a balance between being involved in their children's lives and allowing them to develop independence. Helicopter parenting can hinder a child's ability to make decisions and solve problems on their own.

5. **Education Pressure:** The pressure to succeed academically and in extracurricular activities can be overwhelming for both parents and children. Striking a balance between academic achievements and overall well-being is a constant challenge.

6. **Economic Pressures:** Economic challenges, including rising education costs and housing expenses, can impact the family's financial stability and contribute to stress within the household.

7. **Diversity and Inclusion:** Families today often face the challenge of navigating issues related to diversity, inclusion, and cultural differences. Parents may need to address topics such as racism, gender identity, and sexual orientation with sensitivity.

8. **Mental Health Awareness:** Recognizing and addressing mental health issues in both parents and children is a growing concern. Stigma around mental health may make it challenging for families to seek help when needed.

9. **Environmental Concerns:** The current generation of parents and children is growing up in a world increasingly impacted by environmental issues. Parents may need to address concerns related to climate change, environmental sustainability, and conservation.

10. **Balancing Work and Family:** Achieving a healthy work-life balance can be a significant challenge for parents. The need to meet work demands while being present for family activities and events requires careful navigation.

11. **Peer Pressure and Influences:** Children may face peer pressure and external influences that can impact their behaviour, values, and decision-making. Parents need to equip their children with the skills to make positive choices.

Navigating these challenges requires open communication, adaptability, and a supportive environment for both parents and children. Seeking professional guidance when needed and fostering a strong family bond can contribute to overcoming these challenges in the parenting process.

Road Map for Parenting Excursion:

We strive to make Parenting easier and more enjoyable via following activity-based modules, in the lap of nature, through our Professionals design activities, keeping all psychological and scientific factors in mind.

Understanding Different Parenting Styles and Approaches

Parenting styles and approaches can vary widely, reflecting differences in cultural backgrounds, family structures, personal beliefs, and individual personalities. Here are 15 different styles and approaches to parenting, each with a brief explanation and an illustrative example:

1. **Authoritative Parenting:** This style is characterized by high responsiveness and high demands. Authoritative parents set clear rules and guidelines but are also responsive to their children's needs and open to dialogue.

   - **Example**: A parent allows their child to have a say in their bedtime routine, but maintains a consistent bedtime to ensure the child gets enough sleep.

2. **Authoritarian Parenting:** Known for high demands and low responsiveness, authoritarian parents enforce strict rules and expect obedience without question.

- **Example:** A parent imposes a strict rule of no television on weekdays, with no room for discussion or exceptions.

3. **Permissive Parenting:** Permissive parents are highly responsive but make few demands. They are lenient and often act more like friends than traditional authority figures.
- **Example:** A parent lets their child decide what they want to eat for every meal, even if it means having ice cream for dinner.

4. **Uninvolved Parenting:** Uninvolved parents are low in both responsiveness and demands. They may fulfil basic needs but are generally detached from their child's life.
- **Example:** A parent is unaware of their child's school schedule or homework assignments and rarely attends school events.

5. **Helicopter Parenting:** Helicopter parents are overly focused on their children's experiences and problems, often micromanaging their lives.
- **Example:** A parent constantly checks in with their college-aged child to manage their schedule, coursework, and social engagements.

6. **Gaslighting Parenting:** Gaslighting in parenting refers to a harmful approach in which a parent intentionally or unintentionally manipulates their child's perception, emotions, or reality to control or undermine them.
- Example: Feelings dismissal Child: "I feel sad because my friend didn't invite me to their birthday party." Gaslighting Response: "Don't be ridiculous. You're just overly emotional. It's not a big deal."

7. **Attachment Parenting:** This approach emphasizes the formation of a strong emotional bond with the child, often through physical closeness and responsiveness to needs.
- **Example:** A parent practices co-sleeping and baby-wearing to maintain close physical proximity to their infant.

8. **Positive Parenting:** Positive parenting focuses on encouraging good behaviour through positive reinforcement and guidance rather than punishment.

- **Example:** A parent rewards their child with extra playtime for completing homework on time instead of punishing them for procrastination.

9. **Tiger Parenting:** A term often associated with some Asian cultures, tiger parenting is strict or demanding, pushing children to attain high levels of academic achievement or success in extracurricular activities.

- **Example:** A parent enrolls their child in several after-school tutoring programs and expects top grades in all subjects.

10. **Free-Range Parenting:** This approach encourages children to function independently and with minimal parental supervision, within reasonable boundaries of safety and common sense.

- **Example:** A parent allows their young child to walk to the neighbourhood park alone to play with friends.

11. Democratic Parenting: Democratic parents encourage their children to participate in family decision-making processes, promoting a sense of responsibility and independence.

- **Example:** A family holds a weekly meeting where each member, including the children, can voice opinions and vote on family activities.

12. **Mindful Parenting:** Mindful parenting involves being emotionally aware and present in interactions with children, responding to their needs thoughtfully rather than reactively.

- **Example:** A parent notices their own frustration rising during a child's tantrum and takes a moment to breathe and calm down before responding.

13. **Holistic Parenting:** Holistic parenting looks at the child's overall well-being, including physical, emotional, spiritual, and intellectual development, often incorporating alternative health practices.

- **Example:** A parent chooses organic foods, limits screen time, and uses natural remedies for health care.

14. **Nurturant Parenting:** This style focuses on nurturing and caring for children's emotional and physical needs with empathy and warmth.

- **Example:** A parent consistently offers hugs, comforting words, and reassurance during times of stress or disappointment for the child.

15. **Co-Parenting:** Co-parenting involves parents who are separated or divorced but work together to raise their children in a cooperative and supportive manner.

- **Example:** Divorced parents maintain a consistent schedule and rules for their children, communicating regularly about their children's needs and activities.

16. **Parallel Parenting:** In situations where co-parenting is not possible due to high conflict, parallel parenting allows each parent to have a separate relationship with the child, minimizing direct interaction between the parents.

- **Example:** Each parent attends separate parent-teacher conferences and hosts separate birthday parties for the child to avoid conflict.

Each of these parenting styles and approaches has its own set of practices, beliefs, and outcomes, and parents may find themselves using a combination of these styles depending on the situation and the individual needs of their children.

Knowing, Understanding and Accepting The Child and Their Feelings.

Story: "The Garden of Understanding"

Part 1: The Blossoming Garden

In the bustling village of Aasha, nestled at the foothills of the Himalayas, lived a lively boy named Akshaj. His boundless curiosity and infectious laughter were the heart of his family. Akshaj's parents, Rohan and Meera, juggled work and household chores, often finding themselves exhausted by the end of the day. Despite their busyness, they always made time for Akshaj, understanding the importance of nurturing his growing mind and heart.

One day, Akshaj trudged home from school, his usual sparkle dimmed. His teacher had scolded him for a misunderstood mistake, and he felt a heavy cloud of sadness hanging over him. Rohan, noticing Akshaj's unusual quietness, suggested, "How about we visit the old banyan tree near the river?"

Akshaj nodded, and soon they were walking along the forest path, the sounds of chirping birds and rustling leaves surrounding them. Rohan practiced active listening, bending down to Akshaj's level, making eye contact, and asking, "What's on your mind, champ?"

With the comfort of his father's attention and the serenity of nature, Akshaj began to open up. He spoke of the day's events, his frustrations, and his feelings of unfairness. Rohan listened intently, reflecting back Akshaj's words to ensure he understood. "I see, you felt upset because you were misunderstood," he said gently.

As they walked, they reached a clearing where wildflowers bloomed in vibrant colours. Rohan had an idea. "Let's plant our own little garden here, a place where we can come whenever we need to talk or feel better."

Akshaj's eyes lit up, and they began to dig and plant, sowing seeds of marigolds and sunflowers. Through this activity, Rohan taught Akshaj about empathy and responsibility, comparing the care of plants to understanding each other's feelings.

Each evening, after school, Akshaj and his parents would visit their garden. They shared stories, laughed, and sometimes just sat in silence, enjoying the peace. Meera encouraged open communication by asking open-ended questions like, "How did that make you feel?" and shared her own experiences, making Akshaj feel heard and understood.

Under the shade of the old banyan tree, they began a new tradition of journaling. Akshaj would write about his thoughts and emotions, and his parents would do the same. This ritual helped Akshaj process his feelings and strengthened the bond within the family.

Through these practices, Akshaj learned to express his emotions freely. He felt confident and secure, knowing that his parents understood and accepted him. The garden flourished, just like Akshaj's emotional well-being, becoming a sanctuary of understanding and love.

Part 2: The Withering Garden

In the nearby village of Nirasha, lived a boy named Rishi. His life was a mirror image of Akshaj's, but with one stark difference—his parents, Ajay and Suman, were often too preoccupied with their own lives to notice Rishi's emotional needs.

One afternoon, Rishi came home from school, his shoulders slumped and eyes downcast. His teacher had reprimanded him in front of the class, and he felt embarrassed and misunderstood. When he tried to talk to his parents about it, they brushed him off. "Stop whining and focus on your studies," his father said, not looking up from his work.

Rishi's feelings were often dismissed, leaving him no outlet to express his emotions. He felt isolated and struggled with his self-esteem. His parents imposed high expectations on him without considering his individuality or providing a safe space for him to share his thoughts.

Without active listening, empathy, or open communication, Rishi grew distant from his parents. He often saw Akshaj and his family tending to their garden, their laughter and conversations filling the air with warmth. Rishi longed for such understanding and connection but felt trapped in a cycle of neglect.

One evening, as the sun set, Rishi wandered to the edge of the forest and found Akshaj's Garden. He saw the vibrant flowers, the carefully tended plants, and the journal entries under the banyan tree. He realized what he was missing—a space where he could feel understood and accepted.

Conclusion: The Power of Understanding

The story of Akshaj and Rishi highlights the profound impact of knowing, understanding, and accepting a child's feelings. Akshaj's parents created a nurturing environment through active listening, empathy, and open communication, allowing Akshaj to flourish. In contrast, Rishi's parents, who neglected these practices, unintentionally caused emotional harm and isolation. This tale serves as a powerful reminder of the importance of being present, non-judgmental, and supportive in parenting. By fostering a garden of understanding, parents can help their children grow into emotionally healthy and resilient individuals. The story of Akshaj's blossoming garden and Rishi's withering one underscores the vital role of love, empathy, and open communication in nurturing a child's heart and mind.

Knowing, understanding and accepting the child and their feelings.

Certainly! Knowing, understanding, and accepting your child and their feelings is crucial for building a strong parent-child relationship. Here are some techniques that may help:

2. **Active Listening:**
- Pay full attention when your child talks to you.
- Make eye contact and put away distractions like phones.
- Reflect back what you've heard to ensure understanding.
- **Nature-Based Activity:** Take a nature walk together. Use this time to talk and share your thoughts and feelings while being surrounded by the calming influence of nature.
- **Advantages:** Builds trust, enhances communication skills, and helps your child feel heard and valued.
- This provides an opportunity for open communication. Active listening fosters trust and helps children feel heard and understood.

3. **Empathy Building:**
- Try to understand things from your child's perspective.
- Acknowledge their feelings without judgment.
- Use phrases like "I understand," or "I can see how that would make you feel..."
- **Activity:** Share stories from your own experiences to help them see that you understand similar feelings. For example, "I remember feeling scared too when..."

- **Nature Activity:** Plant a garden together.
- **Practical Activity:** Role-playing scenarios where you take on your child's role can help you better understand their experiences.
- **Advantages:** Fosters emotional connection, promotes understanding, and helps in problem-solving.
- Caring for plants & nature can teach empathy, responsibility, and the importance of nurturing. Use this time to discuss emotions and how they can be similar to caring for living things

4. **Open Communication:**
- Create an environment where your child feels comfortable expressing their thoughts and emotions.
- Encourage them to share their feelings without fear of judgement & punishment.
- **Activity:** Use "feeling" words and ask open-ended questions. For instance, "How did that make you feel?" instead of "Did you have a good day?"
- **Activity:** Share your feelings with your child and explain how you cope with various emotions. This helps normalize the expression of feelings.
- **Advantages:** Encourages openness, reduces fear of judgment, and strengthens the parent-child bond.

5. **Journaling:**
- **Technique:** Encourage your child to keep a journal to record their thoughts and feelings. Reviewing the journal together can facilitate open communication.
- **Nature-Based Activity:** Choose a quiet outdoor spot for journaling. Being in nature can inspire reflection and introspection. (a recording of thoughts, experiences, and observations that have been written down) Sit by a stream or under a tree and journal together.

- Engage in Screen-Free Activities Together: Spend quality time without screens, like playing board games or cooking together.

4. **Create Tech-Free Zones:**
- Designate specific areas in the house where technology is not allowed, like bedrooms or the dining table.
- Dining Table Rule: Make mealtimes screen-free to encourage family conversations.
- Bedroom Rule: Avoid screens in bedrooms to improve sleep quality.

5. **Family Screen Time – Creating a family plan:**
- Engage in screen time together, such as watching educational programs or playing interactive games.
- Involve the Family: Discuss and establish screen time limits collaboratively with your children. Make it a family decision, Discuss and decide together on reasonable durations for different activities.
- Consistency is Key: Implement consistent rules and expectations across all devices and family members.

6. **Establish Tech-Free Times:**
- Unplug Before Bed: Create a tech-free bedtime routine to improve sleep quality.
- Family Time Without Screens: Designate specific hours or days for family activities without screens.

7. **Set Screen time limit Use Parental Controls:**
- Use Parental Controls: Set up controls on devices to limit access during specific hours and access to inappropriate content and set time restrictions.
- Time Management Apps: Install apps that track and limit screen time.

8. Highlight Real-life Experiences:
- Share stories or examples of enjoyable real-life experiences that can be missed if too much time is spent on screens, such as playing with friends, exploring nature, or pursuing hobbies

9. Model Healthy Behaviour:
- Demonstrate responsible technology use, and children are likely to follow suit.

10. Encourage Offline Activities:
- Promote hobbies, sports, reading, and other non-digital activities to balance screen time.
- Team Sports: Enrol children in team sports or individual physical activities.
- Family Fitness: Plan family fitness routines or outdoor games.

4. Tips:

1. Establish a Routine:
- Create a daily schedule that includes designated times for homework, chores, and recreational activities.

2. Communicate with Children:
- Discuss the reasons behind screen time limits and involve children in setting boundaries.

3. Provide Alternatives:
- Offer engaging offline activities to replace excessive screen time.

4. Monitor and Adjust:
- Assess Progress: Regularly evaluate the impact of reduced screen time on your child's behavior and well-being.
- Adjust Accordingly: Modify your approach based on feedback and the child's evolving needs.

5. Celebrate Achievements:

- Positive Reinforcement: Acknowledge and reward efforts to reduce screen time and engage in nature-based activities.
- Celebrate Milestones: Recognize and celebrate milestones in your child's outdoor exploration and play.

6. Monitor Content:

- Be aware of the content your child is consuming, and discuss appropriate and inappropriate materials.

5. Guidelines:

a. Engage in Joint Activities: Participate in activities that involve face-to-face interaction, such as board games, family outings, or art projects.

b. Promote Reading: Encourage reading physical books instead of using digital devices.

c. Limit Social Media: Establish age-appropriate rules for social media usage and monitor online activities.

d. Educational Screen Time: Allow screen time for educational purposes, and choose high-quality, age-appropriate content.

6. Advantages:

1. Improved Physical Health:

- Reduced screen time can lead to increased physical activity and healthier lifestyles.

2. Discovering the World:

- Talk about the excitement of exploring the real world, discovering new plants, animals, and landscapes. Nature is full of surprises!

3. Building Friendships:

- Outdoor play helps in making new friends and strengthening existing friendships. They can share laughs and create wonderful memories together.

4. **Enhanced Sleep:**
- Less screen time, especially before bedtime, can improve sleep quality.

5. **Better Social Skills:**
- Face-to-face interactions are crucial for the development of social skills, empathy, and communication.

6. **Increased Creativity:**
- Non-digital activities stimulate creativity and imagination.

7. **Improved Academic Performance:**
- Balanced screen time allows for more time for homework and other educational activities.

7. **Monitoring and Adaptation:**

1. **Regularly Assess and Adjust:**
- Periodically evaluate the effectiveness of your approach and make adjustments based on your child's development and changing needs.

2. **Stay Informed:**
- Keep abreast of new technologies and trends to make informed decisions about your child's screen time.

Remember that each child is unique, and the key is to find a balance that works for your family. Open communication and flexibility are essential in adapting to the changing needs of your child as they grow.

Inculcating Value of Money

Story: "Vihan's Journey to Financial Wisdom"

In a small village in India, nestled among green fields and flowing rivers, lived a young boy named Vihan. Vihan was curious and energetic, always eager to explore the world around him. His parents, understanding the importance of financial wisdom, decided it was time to teach him the value of money through various engaging activities.

Allowance and Budgeting

One sunny morning, Vihan's father handed him a small pouch of coins. "This is your allowance for the month," he said. "Let's create a budget together." They sat down and divided the money into three jars: one for spending, one for saving, and one for sharing with those in need. Vihan learned to allocate his money wisely, ensuring he had enough for his favourite sweets, savings for a new cricket bat, and a portion to help a friend in need.

Key Takeaway: Budgeting teaches children to make thoughtful decisions and plan for the future.

Shopping and Price Comparison

On their next trip to the market, Vihan's mother encouraged him to compare prices. She explained how some stalls offered discounts while others sold items at higher prices. Vihan enjoyed the challenge of finding the best deals, learning to make smart purchasing decisions and save money.

Key Takeaway: Price comparison develops critical thinking and money-saving habits.

Saving Jar

Back at home, Vihan's father gave him a transparent jar for his savings. They set a goal to save enough for a special toy. Each week, Vihan eagerly watched his savings grow, understanding the joy of delayed gratification.

Key Takeaway: Saving reinforces discipline and the benefits of waiting for something valuable.

Entrepreneurial Ventures

One day, inspired by a story he heard in school, Vihan decided to start a small business. With his parents' guidance, he set up a lemonade stand. He learned about profits, expenses, and reinvestment, and was thrilled to see his hard work pay off.

Key Takeaway: Entrepreneurship fosters creativity, financial understanding, and independence.

Needs vs. Wants

During a family discussion, Vihan's parents helped him create a list of needs and wants. They categorized items like food and clothes as needs, and toys and games as wants. This activity taught Vihan to prioritize his spending and avoid impulsive purchases.

Key Takeaway: Differentiating between needs and wants cultivates a sense of prioritization and mindful spending.

Financial Board Games

On rainy days, the family played financial board games like Monopoly. Vihan enjoyed the game, unaware that he was learning valuable lessons about money management, strategic thinking, and basic math skills.

Key Takeaway: Board games make learning about money enjoyable and educational.

Goal Setting

Vihan's parents encouraged him to set short-term and long-term financial goals. Together, they discussed the steps needed to achieve these goals, teaching Vihan the importance of planning and perseverance.

Key Takeaway: Goal setting instils the value of planning and working towards objectives.

Open Discussions about Money

Vihan's family believed in transparency. They had open, age-appropriate discussions about family finances, including income, expenses, and saving strategies. These conversations prepared Vihan for real-world financial responsibilities.

Key Takeaway: Open discussions about money foster understanding and preparedness for financial responsibilities.

Nature Scavenger Hunt for Budgeting

One weekend, Vihan's parents organized a nature scavenger hunt in the nearby park. They gave him a budget to find specific items within the park. This activity taught Vihan to budget, prioritize, and make wise spending choices.

Key Takeaway: Budgeting activities in nature enhance decision-making skills.

Gardening for Patience and Delayed Gratification

Vihan and his father started a small garden. They planted seeds and cared for the plants daily. Vihan learned patience and responsibility, understanding that just like saving money, nurturing plants required time and effort before reaping the rewards.

Key Takeaway: Gardening teaches patience, responsibility, and the concept of delayed gratification.

Nature-based Crafts for Resourcefulness

Using materials found in nature, Vihan created beautiful crafts. His parents explained how resourcefulness in crafts is similar to managing money responsibly. Vihan learned to value resources and think creatively.

Key Takeaway: Resourcefulness in crafts parallels responsible money management.

Outdoor Market Simulation for Money Management

Vihan's parents set up a pretend outdoor market. He practiced buying and selling natural items, learning the basics of trading, negotiation, and understanding the value of goods. This simulation introduced him to the dynamics of supply and demand.

Key Takeaway: Market simulations introduce fundamental concepts of trade and value.

Nature Journaling for Goal Setting

Vihan maintained a nature journal, noting his observations and setting nature-related goals. His parents linked this practice to saving money for specific purposes, teaching him to track progress and achieve goals.

Key Takeaway: Journaling promotes goal setting and tracking progress.

Nature Camping for Resource Conservation

During a camping trip, Vihan learned about conservation and responsible resource use. His parents discussed how saving money aligns with conserving resources and making mindful choices.

Key Takeaway: Camping fosters environmental consciousness and frugality.

Nature Exploration for Value Appreciation

On their nature walks, Vihan's parents discussed the intrinsic value of the environment. They explained that not everything valuable can be measured in money, teaching Vihan to appreciate both material and non-material aspects of life.

Key Takeaway: Understanding intrinsic value promotes a balanced perspective on money and life.

Conclusion

Through these activities, Vihan learned invaluable lessons about the value of money, resourcefulness, and the importance of making wise financial decisions. These experiences prepared him for a future of financial responsibility and well-being.

Key Takeaways

1. **Budgeting and Allowance:** Teach children to allocate money for spending, saving, and sharing.

2. **Price Comparison:** Develop critical thinking and money-saving habits.

3. **Saving:** Reinforce discipline and delayed gratification.

4. **Entrepreneurship:** Foster creativity and financial understanding.

5. **Needs vs. Wants:** Cultivate prioritization and mindful spending.

6. **Financial Games:** Make learning about money enjoyable and educational.

7. **Goal Setting:** Instill planning and perseverance.

8. **Open Discussions:** Foster understanding and preparedness for financial responsibilities.

9. **Budgeting Activities:** Enhance decision-making skills in practical settings.

10. **Gardening:** Teach patience, responsibility, and delayed gratification.

11. **Crafts:** Promote resourcefulness and responsible money management.

12. **Market Simulations:** Introduce trade and value dynamics.

13. **Journaling:** Encourage goal setting and tracking progress.

14. **Camping:** Foster environmental consciousness and frugality.

15. **Nature Appreciation:** Promote a balanced perspective on money and life.

Inculcating Value of Money

Inculcating the value of money in children is an important aspect of parenting that can contribute to their financial well-being and responsible behaviour in the future. Here are some activities-based techniques along with their respective advantages and tips to teach kids the value of money:

1. **Allowance and Budgeting:**
- **Activity:** Give your child a weekly or monthly allowance and help them create a budget. Encourage them to allocate money for spending, saving, and sharing.
- **Advantages:** Teaches budgeting skills, decision-making, and the importance of saving for future goals.

2. **Shopping and Price Comparison:**
- **Activity:** Involve your child in grocery shopping. Teach them to compare prices, look for discounts, and make smart purchasing decisions.

- **Advantages:** Develops critical thinking, decision-making, and money-saving habits.

3. **Saving Jar:**
- **Activity:** Provide a transparent jar for saving money. Help your child set a savings goal and watch the money accumulate over time.
- **Advantages:** Reinforces the concept of delayed gratification and instils discipline in saving.

4. **Entrepreneurial Ventures:**
- **Activity:** Encourage your child to start a small business, such as a lemonade stand or selling handmade crafts. Discuss profits, expenses, and reinvestment.
- **Advantages:** Promotes creativity, entrepreneurship, and financial understanding.

5. **Needs vs. Wants:**
- **Activity:** Create a list of needs and wants with your child. Discuss and categorize items to help them differentiate between essential and non-essential expenses.
- **Advantages:** Cultivates a sense of prioritization and helps in avoiding impulsive spending.

6. **Financial Board Games:**
- **Activity:** Play board games like Monopoly or The Game of Life that involve money and decision-making.
- **Advantages:** Makes learning about money enjoyable, reinforces basic math skills, and encourages strategic thinking.

7. **Goal Setting:**
- **Activity:** Set short-term and long-term financial goals with your child. Discuss the steps needed to achieve these goals.
- **Advantages:** Teaches the importance of planning, perseverance, and the value of achieving financial objectives.

8. Open Discussions about Money:

- **Activity:** Have open and age-appropriate discussions about family finances, including income, expenses, and saving strategies.
- **Advantages:** Fosters transparency, helps kids understand real-world financial situations, and prepares them for financial responsibilities.

9. Nature Scavenger Hunt for Budgeting:

- **Activity:** Organize a scavenger hunt in a park or natural setting where children have to find items within a specified budget.
- **Advantages:** Teaches budgeting, prioritization, and decision-making skills.
- **Tips:** Provide them with a predetermined budget and encourage them to make wise spending choices.

10. Gardening for Patience and Delayed Gratification:

- **Activity:** Start a small garden with your children, involving them in planting, watering, and caring for the plants.
- **Advantages:** Teaches patience, responsibility, and the concept of delayed gratification as they wait for plants to grow.
- **Tips:** Link the growth of plants to saving money and the rewards of waiting for something valuable.

11. Nature-based Crafts for Resourcefulness:

- **Activity:** Engage in nature-based crafts where children use materials found in nature to create art or useful items.
- **Advantages:** Encourages resourcefulness, creativity, and the understanding of the value of repurposing.
- **Tips:** Discuss how using resources wisely in crafts is similar to managing money responsibly.

12. Outdoor Market Simulation for Money Management:

- **Activity:** Set up a pretend outdoor market where kids can "buy" and "sell" natural items.

- **Advantages:** Introduces the basics of trading, negotiation, and understanding the value of goods.
- **Tips:** Assign different values to items, and let them experience the dynamics of supply and demand.

13. Nature Journaling for Goal Setting:
- **Activity:** Encourage children to maintain a nature journal, noting their observations and setting nature-related goals.
- **Advantages:** Promotes goal setting, planning, and tracking progress over time.
- **Tips:** Relate the idea of achieving nature-related goals to the concept of saving money for a specific purpose.

14. Nature Camping for Resource Conservation:
- **Activity:** Plan a camping trip where children learn about conservation, responsible resource use, and the importance of minimalism.
- **Advantages:** Fosters an appreciation for resources, environmental consciousness, and frugality.
- **Tips:** Discuss how saving money aligns with conserving resources and making mindful choices.

15. Nature Exploration for Value Appreciation:
- **Activity:** Take nature walks and discuss the intrinsic value of the environment, including its impact on our well-being.
- **Advantages:** Instils a sense of appreciation for non-material aspects of life and the importance of balance.
- **Tips:** Draw parallels between appreciating nature's intrinsic value and understanding that not everything valuable can be measured in money.

Tips:

Start Early: Introduce money concepts gradually as children grow, adapting activities to their developmental stage.

- **Be a Role Model:** Demonstrate responsible financial behaviour and decision-making to serve as a positive example.
- **Repetition and Reinforcement:** Consistently revisit money-related activities to reinforce lessons and build a strong foundation.
- **Make it Practical:** Relate concepts to real-life situations to enhance understanding and applicability.
- **Encourage Questions:** Create an environment where children feel comfortable asking questions about money matters.

Remember to adapt these activities to your child's age and interests, and use them as opportunities for open discussions about money, values, and responsible behavior. Consistency and positive reinforcement will contribute to the development of a strong financial foundation.

Overcoming Helicopter Parenting Style

Story: The Kite of Independence

In a bustling neighbourhood in Bangalore, lived a family that was the epitome of success and care. Rajesh and Anjali were proud parents of ten-year-old Akshaj, a bright and talented boy. Rajesh, a successful software engineer, and Anjali, a dedicated homemaker, wanted nothing but the best for their son. However, their love and concern often led them to hover over Akshaj, making decisions for him, and shielding him from every potential failure. They were the quintessential helicopter parents.

Akshaj was often found under the watchful eyes of his parents, who would meticulously plan his every move, from his homework schedule to his playtime. While Akshaj excelled in academics, he started feeling a sense of unease, a lack of confidence in making decisions on his own. He began to withdraw, fearing the consequences of stepping out of the safe cocoon his parents had woven around him.

One sunny afternoon, the neighbourhood was abuzz with excitement. It was the annual kite-flying festival, a cherished tradition where families gathered on their rooftops to fly colourful kites, competing to see whose kite would soar the highest. Akshaj had always been fascinated by kites, but Rajesh and Anjali never allowed him to participate, worrying about the dangers of sharp strings and the high terrace walls.

This year, however, Akshaj's friend Rohan, an adventurous and independent boy, convinced Akshaj to join him. Rohan's parents, although caring, encouraged him to explore and learn from his experiences. Akshaj mustered the courage to ask his parents for permission. After much hesitation and persuasion, Rajesh and Anjali reluctantly agreed, but only if they could supervise closely.

As the festival began, Akshaj's excitement was palpable. Rohan taught him how to prepare the kite, tie the string, and control it against the wind. Akshaj's initial attempts were clumsy, but Rohan's patience and guidance helped him improve. Rajesh and Anjali, watching from a distance, were anxious but remained silent, realizing the importance of this moment for Akshaj.

Gradually, Akshaj's kite began to rise, wobbling at first, but then gaining stability. The joy on Akshaj's face was indescribable. He learned to control the kite, feeling a sense of accomplishment and independence he had never experienced before. Rajesh and Anjali watched in awe as their son navigated the challenges of kite flying, solving problems, and making decisions on his own.

As the sun began to set, Akshaj's kite soared high, dancing gracefully against the orange sky. Rajesh and Anjali realized the profound lesson in this simple activity. They saw the confidence blossoming in Akshaj, the spark of independence lighting up his eyes. It dawned on them that their overprotectiveness, though well-intentioned, was holding Akshaj back from realizing his true potential.

From that day on, Rajesh and Anjali made a conscious effort to step back, allowing Akshaj more freedom to explore, make mistakes, and learn from them. They encouraged him to take up responsibilities, join team sports, and engage in activities that fostered problem-solving and independence. Akshaj thrived, becoming more resilient, confident, and self-reliant.

Key Takeaways:

1. **Awareness and Acknowledgment:**
   - Recognize the need for a balance between involvement and allowing space for growth.
   - Understand that overprotectiveness can hinder long-term development.

2. **Trust Your Child:**
   - Trust in your child's ability to handle situations and learn from experiences.
   - Accept that failure is a natural part of the learning process.

3. **Encourage Independence:**
   - Gradually give more responsibilities and opportunities to make decisions.
   - Foster a sense of independence by allowing tasks to be completed on their own.

4. **Set Realistic Expectations:**
   - Be realistic about what is developmentally appropriate.
   - Avoid putting unnecessary pressure to excel in every aspect.

5. **Open Communication:**
   - Encourage open and honest communication about thoughts, feelings, and concerns.
   - Be approachable and non-judgmental.

6. **Teach Problem-Solving Skills:**
   - Guide in developing problem-solving skills rather than solving problems for them.
   - Encourage critical thinking through questions and discussions.

7. **Provide Opportunities for Growth:**
   - Allow participation in extracurricular activities and experiences.
   - Exposure to challenges builds resilience and self-confidence.

8. **Model Healthy Behaviour:**
   - Demonstrate a balanced approach to managing stress and challenges.
   - Show how to handle setbacks with resilience and positivity.

9. **Gradual Independence:**
   - Gradually give more freedom as responsibility and maturity are demonstrated.
   - Provide opportunities for success to build confidence.

10. **Seek Professional Guidance if Needed:**
    - Consider professional support if struggling to overcome helicopter parenting habits.

Activities to Foster Independence:

1. **Outdoor Exploration:** Nature walks, hiking, or camping trips to explore and appreciate the outdoors.

2. **Team Sports:** Enrol in team sports to learn teamwork, resilience, and decision-making.

3. **Cooking and Meal Preparation:** Involve in age-appropriate cooking tasks to develop life skills.

4. **Problem-Solving Board Games:** Games like chess or strategy board games to encourage critical thinking.

5. **Building and Crafting:** Activities like building with blocks or crafting to enhance creativity and problem-solving.

6. **Responsibility Chart:** Create a chart for daily tasks to encourage responsibility.

7. **Volunteer Work:** Engage in volunteer activities to develop empathy and perspective.

8. **Time Management Activities:** Use a schedule or planner to organize time efficiently.

9. **Self-Directed Learning:** Encourage pursuing interests and passions independently.

10. **Reflective Conversations:** Have discussions about decisions, consequences, and problem-solving.

Through the kite-flying festival, Akshaj and his parents learned the value of balance in parenting. By stepping back and allowing room for growth, they nurtured Akshaj's independence, preparing him to navigate life's challenges with confidence and resilience.

Overcoming Helicopter Parenting Style

Helicopter parenting refers to a style of parenting where parents are overly involved in their child's life, constantly monitoring and hovering over them. While it may stem from good intentions, such as ensuring the child's safety and success, it can have drawbacks and hinder the child's development of independence and problem-solving skills. Here are some tips to overcome helicopter parenting and its respective advantages:

1. Awareness and Acknowledgment:

- Recognize that helicopter parenting may not be in the best interest of your child's long-term development.

- Acknowledge the need for a balance between being involved and allowing your child space to grow.

2. Trust Your Child:

- Trust your child's ability to make decisions and handle situations. Allow them to learn from their mistakes and experiences.

- Understand that failure is a natural part of the learning process and can contribute to personal growth.

3. Encourage Independence:

- Gradually give your child more responsibilities and opportunities to make decisions based on their age and maturity level.
- Foster a sense of independence by allowing them to complete tasks on their own.

4. Set Realistic Expectations:

- Be realistic about what your child can achieve and what is developmentally appropriate for their age.
- Avoid putting unnecessary pressure on them to excel in every aspect of life.

5. Open Communication:

- Establish open and honest communication with your child. Encourage them to express their thoughts, feelings, and concerns.
- Be approachable and non-judgmental so that they feel comfortable discussing their experiences with you.

6. Teach Problem-Solving Skills:

- Instead of solving problems for your child, guide them in developing problem-solving skills.
- Encourage critical thinking by asking questions that help them analyse situations and come up with solutions.

7. Provide Opportunities for Growth:

- Allow your child to participate in extracurricular activities and experiences that promote personal and social development.
- Exposure to challenges can build resilience and self-confidence.

8. Model Healthy Behaviour:

- Demonstrate a balanced and healthy approach to managing stress and challenges.

- Show your child how to handle setbacks and disappointments with resilience and a positive attitude.

9. Gradual Independence:

- Gradually give your child more freedom as they demonstrate responsibility and maturity.
- Provide opportunities for them to experience success and build confidence in their abilities.

10. Seek Professional Guidance if Needed: - If you find it challenging to break the helicopter parenting habit, consider seeking guidance from a parenting coach or counsellor. - Professional support can provide strategies tailored to your specific situation.

1. Outdoor Exploration:

- Nature walks, hiking, or camping trips allow children to explore and appreciate the outdoors.
- Teach them basic navigation skills, like reading maps or using a compass.

2. Team Sports:

- Enrol your child in team sports where they can learn to work with others, follow instructions from a coach, and make decisions on the field.
- Team activities also teach resilience and the importance of effort and practice.

3. Cooking and Meal Preparation:

- Involve your child in age-appropriate cooking tasks. Gradually give them more responsibilities in the kitchen.
- This helps them develop essential life skills and boosts their confidence.

4. **Problem-Solving Board Games:**
   - Games like chess, Scrabble, or strategy board games encourage critical thinking and decision-making.
   - Allow your child to make choices and experience the consequences within the game's context.

5. **Building and Crafting:**
   - Activities like building with blocks, Legos, or crafting projects can enhance creativity and problem-solving.
   - Encourage them to plan and execute their own projects.

6. **Responsibility Chart:**
   - Create a chart outlining daily tasks and responsibilities. Allow your child to take charge of certain tasks, such as setting the table or feeding pets.
   - Reinforce the importance of completing tasks independently.

7. **Volunteer Work:**
   - Engaging in volunteer activities exposes children to different perspectives and helps them develop empathy.
   - Choose age-appropriate volunteer opportunities where they can contribute meaningfully.

8. **Time Management Activities:**
   - Provide a schedule or planner and help your child organize their time for homework, play, and other activities.
   - Teach them the value of planning and managing time efficiently.

9. **Self-Directed Learning:**
   - Encourage your child to pursue their interests and passions. Allow them to choose books, projects, or activities related to their hobbies.
   - This fosters a sense of autonomy and self-motivation.

10. Reflective Conversations:

- Have open and honest discussions about decisions, consequences, and problem-solving.

- Encourage your child to express their thoughts and feelings, promoting self-awareness.

Remember, the goal is to raise independent, resilient individuals who can navigate the challenges of life. Striking a balance between support and allowing room for growth is crucial for a child's overall development.

Top of Form

Overcoming helicopter parenting behavior involves gradually fostering independence and self-reliance in children. Incorporating activities and games that encourage autonomy, decision-making, and problem-solving can be effective. Here are some suggestions:

Remember, the key is gradual progression. Start with activities that align with your child's current level of independence and gradually introduce more challenges as they become comfortable. Be patient and supportive, praising their efforts and achievements along the way.

Understanding Gaslighting Parenting Approach

Understanding Gaslighting Parenting Approach

Gaslighting parenting is an unhealthy and harmful approach to raising children in which parents or caregivers manipulate their child's perception of reality, emotions, or experiences. This can have long-lasting negative effects on a child's self-esteem, emotional well-being, and relationships.

Gaslighting in parenting refers to a harmful approach in which a parent intentionally or unintentionally manipulates their child's perception, emotions, or reality to control or undermine them. Here are some simple illustrative examples of gaslighting in parenting:

1. **Denying a Child's Feelings:**
- Example: A child says, "I'm scared of the dark." The parent responds, "Don't be silly; there's nothing to be afraid of. You're not scared."
- Importance: Gaslighting in this context can make the child doubt their own emotions and instincts, potentially leading to anxiety and a lack of emotional self-regulation.

2. **Shifting Blame:**
- Example: A parent accidentally breaks a toy, and when the child points it out, the parent says, "You must have done something to make it break."
- Importance: This can make the child feel responsible for things that aren't their fault and may erode their sense of trust and safety within the family.

3. **Withholding Love and Approval:**
- Example: A child brings home a good report card, but the parent responds with indifference and says, "Well, it's not perfect. You can do better."
- Importance: This form of gaslighting can undermine a child's self-esteem and create a constant need for external validation.

4. **Minimizing Feelings:**
- Example: A child is upset because a friend excluded them from a game, and the parent dismisses it by saying, "It's not a big deal. Stop overreacting."
- Importance: This can teach the child to suppress their emotions, hindering their ability to express and process feelings in a healthy way.

5. **Projection:**
- Example: A parent often displays anger and then accuses the child of being overly aggressive, saying, "You're always so angry; it's exhausting!"
- Importance: This can confuse the child and make them internalize negative traits projected onto them by the parent.

It is essential for parents to avoid gaslighting because it can harm a child's emotional development, self-esteem, and overall mental well-being. Instead, healthy parenting involves fostering trust, open communication, empathy, and validation of a child's feelings and experiences.

Story: "A Journey to Truth"

In a small village in the foothills of the Himalayas, a young boy named Akshaj lived with his parents. His father, Rajesh, was a respected school teacher, and his mother, Meera, was known for her beautiful garden. Akshaj loved exploring the forests and rivers around his home, but he often felt confused and doubted his own feelings and experiences due to his father's constant dismissals and manipulations.

One sunny afternoon, Akshaj came home excited after finding a rare bird during his nature walk. "Papa, I saw a beautiful golden pheasant today!" he exclaimed.

Rajesh, without looking up from his newspaper, replied, "Akshaj, you must be mistaken. There are no golden pheasants here. You probably saw something else."

Akshaj's heart sank. This wasn't the first time his father had dismissed his experiences. He remembered another time when he had told his father about his fear of the dark, only to be told, "Don't be silly. You're not scared."

As days passed, Akshaj began to doubt his own perceptions and feelings. His mother, Meera, noticed the change in her son. She saw how Rajesh's dismissals and manipulations affected Akshaj's confidence and self-esteem.

Determined to help her son, Meera decided to introduce nature-based activities to rebuild Akshaj's trust in himself and to strengthen their bond. She started with a simple Feelings and Emotions Game. They used cards with different facial expressions and talked about times when they felt those emotions.

"Akshaj, can you tell me about a time when you felt happy?" Meera asked gently.

Akshaj thought for a moment and said, "I felt happy when I saw the golden pheasant."

Meera smiled and validated his feeling, "That sounds wonderful, Akshaj. Seeing such a beautiful bird must have been an amazing experience."

Encouraged by his mother's support, Akshaj participated in more activities. They played the Mirror Game, where they mimicked each other's expressions, fostering empathy and understanding. They also engaged in Storytelling and Perspective-Taking, where they read stories and discussed the characters' emotions and challenges, helping Akshaj see different perspectives.

One evening, they went for a Nature Walk. As they walked through the forest, Meera encouraged Akshaj to share his thoughts and feelings. "Akshaj, what do you think about when you see these trees and hear the birds?"

Akshaj opened up, "I feel peaceful and happy, Ma. It's like the forest understands me."

Meera listened attentively, showing empathy and validating his feelings. This open communication helped Akshaj rebuild his trust in himself and his perceptions.

Meera also introduced Positive Reinforcement. She praised Akshaj for his accomplishments and efforts, no matter how small. "You did a great job finding those plants for our garden, Akshaj. I'm so proud of you."

One night, they decided to go Stargazing. Lying on a blanket under the vast night sky, they identified constellations and talked about the universe. Akshaj asked, "Ma, do you think there are other worlds out there?"

Meera smiled and replied, "The universe is full of wonders, Akshaj. Your curiosity and imagination are special. Never stop believing in what you see and feel."

Through these nature-based activities, Akshaj's confidence and self-esteem grew. He learned to trust his own experiences and emotions. Meera's support and validation helped him overcome the negative effects of gaslighting.

Key Takeaways:

1. **Trust and Validation:** It's crucial to validate a child's feelings and experiences, helping them build self-trust and emotional intelligence.

2. **Open Communication:** Encouraging open and honest conversations fosters a strong parent-child bond and promotes emotional well-being.

3. **Positive Reinforcement:** Praising and acknowledging a child's efforts and achievements boost their self-esteem and confidence.

4. **Nature-Based Activities:** Engaging in activities like nature walks, stargazing, and storytelling can create a nurturing environment for children to express themselves freely and confidently.

By embracing these principles, parents can counteract the harmful effects of gaslighting and nurture a healthy, trusting relationship with their children, allowing them to grow into confident and emotionally secure individuals.

To counteract this approach and promote healthy parent-child relationships, nature-based activities and games can be highly effective. These activities encourage open communication, emotional connection, and a sense of trust between parents and children. Here are ten nature-based activities or games, along with their importance and tips for implementing them:

1. **Feelings and Emotions Game:**
- **Importance:** This game helps children recognize and express their emotions, fostering emotional intelligence and self-awareness.

- **Activity:** Use cards or pictures of different facial expressions to teach children about various emotions (happy, sad, angry, etc.). Ask the child to identify and discuss times when they felt those emotions.
- **Tips:** Encourage open and non-judgmental communication. Validate their feelings and let them know it's okay to feel a range of emotions.

2. **Mirror Game:**
- **Importance:** This game builds empathy and helps children understand that their emotions are valid and shared by others.
- **Activity:** Sit facing each other with a mirror in hand or a piece of paper. Take turns making facial expressions, and the child mimics your expression.
- **Tips:** Use this game to teach empathy by discussing how people feel when they make certain expressions. Connect it to real-life situations.

3. **Storytelling and Perspective-Taking:**
- **Importance:** Encourages children to see different perspectives and understand that their experiences are unique.
- **Activity:** Read a story together or make up a story where characters experience different emotions and challenges. Ask the child to imagine how each character feels and why.
- **Tips:** Discuss the characters' emotions and relate them to the child's own experiences. Encourage them to share their thoughts and feelings.

4. **Empowerment Activities:**
- **Importance:** Builds the child's self-esteem and confidence.
- **Activity:** Engage in activities that allow the child to make choices and decisions, such as planning a family outing, decorating their room, or choosing their clothes.

- **Tips:** Provide guidance and support, but also respect their choices. This helps the child develop a sense of autonomy and self-assuredness.

5. **Communication and Active Listening:**
- **Importance:** Encourages open and honest communication between parent and child.
- **Activity:** Set aside dedicated "talk time" with your child, where you actively listen without judgment. Use active listening techniques like reflecting back what they've said.
- **Tips:** Avoid interrupting or dismissing their feelings. Show empathy and validate their experiences.

6. **Positive Reinforcement:**
- **Importance:** Fosters a sense of security and trust in the parent-child relationship.
- **Activity:** Praise and reward your child for their accomplishments and efforts, no matter how small.
- **Tips:** Offer specific praise and acknowledgment. This helps build their self-esteem and reinforces positive behaviours.

7. **Role Reversal:**
- Sometimes, parents can engage in role reversal activities where the child takes on the role of the parent, and the parent takes on the role of the child. This can help parents gain insight into their child's perspective and feelings.

8. **Emotion Cards:**
- Create emotion cards with various emotions written on them (e.g., happy, sad, angry, confused). Sit down with your child and ask them to pick a card that matches how they're feeling. Encourage them to describe why they feel that way, and validate their emotions without judgment.

9. **Nature Walks:**
- **Importance:** Nature walks provide an opportunity for bonding, exploration, and open conversations in a relaxed environment.
- **Tips:** Encourage your child to ask questions, share observations, and discuss their thoughts and feelings while walking in nature. Listen attentively and avoid judgment.

10. **Campfire Stories:**
- **Importance:** Sharing stories around a campfire fosters creativity, trust, and emotional expression.
- **Tips:** Encourage your child to tell stories, both real and imaginary, and participate by sharing your own. Create a safe and non-judgmental atmosphere.

11. **Nature Art and Craft:**
- **Importance:** Creative activities in nature promote self-expression and self-esteem while strengthening the parent-child bond.
- **Tips:** Collect natural materials like leaves, sticks, and rocks to create art together. Praise your child's creativity and encourage them to experiment.

12. **Birdwatching:**
- **Importance:** Birdwatching teaches patience, observation, and appreciation for wildlife while sparking conversations.
- **Tips:** Bring binoculars, a bird guidebook, and a notebook to jot down observations. Discuss the characteristics and behaviours of the birds you encounter.

13. **Nature Scavenger Hunt:**
- **Importance:** Scavenger hunts promote teamwork, problem-solving, and connection with the natural environment.
- **Tips:** Create a list of items or natural features to find, and explore together. Celebrate each discovery, and discuss why each item is important in nature.

14. Planting and Gardening:

- **Importance:** Gardening instils responsibility, patience, and a sense of nurturing in children.

- **Tips:** Assign your child specific gardening tasks and let them take ownership. Discuss the growth process and the importance of caring for living things.

15. Nature Journaling:

- **Importance:** Journaling encourages self-reflection, emotional expression, and connection with nature.

- **Tips:** Provide your child with a journal and encourage them to write or draw their thoughts and experiences in nature. Share your own journal entries as well.

16. Stargazing:

- **Importance:** Stargazing encourages curiosity about the universe and provides opportunities for deep conversations.

- **Tips:** Use a telescope or stargazing app to identify constellations and planets. Discuss the vastness of space and any questions your child may have.

17. Forest Meditation:

- **Importance:** Meditation in nature promotes emotional awareness, relaxation, and stress reduction.

- **Tips:** Find a peaceful spot in the forest, sit quietly, and guide your child through a meditation practice focused on their senses and connection with the natural world.

18. Rock Balancing:

- **Importance:** Balancing rocks requires concentration, patience, and the appreciation of balance and harmony in nature.

- **Tips:** Collect rocks of different sizes and practice stacking them together. Discuss the importance of balance in both nature and life.

General Tips for All Activities:

- Be present and actively engage with your child during these activities.
- Listen attentively to what your child has to say and validate their feelings and observations.
- Avoid judgment and criticism; instead, offer constructive feedback and encouragement.
- Respect your child's boundaries and preferences; don't force them into activities they are uncomfortable with.
- Celebrate small achievements and milestones during these activities to boost your child's self-esteem.
- Use these activities as opportunities to model healthy communication and problem-solving skills.
- Make these nature-based activities a regular part of your routine to build a strong, trusting parent-child relationship based on mutual respect and understanding.

In all these activities, the key is to create a safe, non-judgmental, and open space for your child to express themselves and develop a positive relationship with you as a parent. Encourage questions, active listening, and mutual respect to counteract any harmful gaslighting tendencies and foster a healthy parent-child dynamic.

Role of Spirituality in Healthy Parenting Style

Story: "A Journey of Spiritual Parenting in the Heart of India"

Story:

In a quaint village in India, nestled between lush green fields and flowing rivers, lived the Sharma family. Raj, a dedicated schoolteacher, and Priya, a compassionate nurse, were the proud parents of two children,

Aarav and Ananya. The Sharma's believed in the power of spirituality to guide their family's values and actions.

Mindfulness and Presence:

One evening, Raj and Priya decided to take their children on a nature walk. As they strolled through the serene landscape, they encouraged Aarav and Ananya to observe the vibrant flowers, listen to the chirping birds, and feel the gentle breeze. They practiced deep breathing, feeling more connected to each other and the world around them. This simple act of mindfulness strengthened their bond, making each moment shared in nature more meaningful.

Flip Side: Without these mindfulness practices, the family might have missed out on these moments of deep connection, leading to feelings of disconnection and stress.

Key Takeaway: Mindfulness enhances the parent-child relationship by fostering presence and connection.

Gratitude Practices:

At home, the Sharma's created a family gratitude jar. Each evening, they would gather around and write down something they were thankful for. Aarav wrote about his new friendship at school, while Ananya expressed gratitude for her mother's comforting hug when she was sad. These moments of sharing gratitude cultivated a positive mindset and appreciation within the family.

Flip Side: Without gratitude practices, the family might have focused on negative aspects of life, leading to a lack of appreciation and increased negativity.

Key Takeaway: Gratitude practices cultivate a positive mindset and reinforce the importance of acknowledging blessings.

Connection with Nature:

The Sharma's loved spending weekends camping under the starry sky. Raj would tell stories about the constellations, and Priya taught the kids about different plants and animals. These experiences instilled a sense of wonder and connection with the natural world, fostering environmental stewardship.

Flip Side: Without these outdoor activities, the family might have missed the opportunity to develop a deep appreciation for nature and environmental responsibility.

Key Takeaway: Connecting with nature fosters a sense of interconnectedness and environmental stewardship.

Values-Based Storytelling:

During bedtime, Raj and Priya shared stories from Indian mythology and folklore, highlighting spiritual and moral values. These stories guided Aarav and Ananya in making positive choices, understanding the importance of honesty, kindness, and bravery.

Flip Side: Without values-based storytelling, children might lack a moral compass, leading to confusion in distinguishing right from wrong.

Key Takeaway: Storytelling helps in transmitting cultural and ethical values, guiding children in making positive choices.

Mind-Body Practices:

Priya introduced simple yoga exercises to her children. Each morning, they practiced together, stretching their bodies and calming their minds. These exercises enhanced their emotional regulation and instilled a sense of inner peace.

Flip Side: Without mind-body practices, the family might experience higher levels of stress and emotional turmoil.

Key Takeaway: Mind-body practices enhance emotional regulation and instil a sense of inner peace.

Community Engagement:

The Sharma's often volunteered at the local orphanage, teaching the children, playing games, and sharing meals. This fostered empathy and compassion in Aarav and Ananya, teaching them the importance of helping others.

Flip Side: Without community engagement, the children might grow up with a limited sense of empathy and social responsibility.

Key Takeaway: Volunteering fosters empathy, compassion, and a sense of responsibility towards others' well-being.

Rituals and Traditions:

Every Sunday, the Sharma's had a family meal where they shared stories, laughed, and connected. These rituals provided a sense of continuity, stability, and shared values.

Flip Side: Without such rituals, the family might struggle to find time to connect, leading to feelings of instability and disconnection.

Key Takeaway: Family rituals establish a sense of continuity, stability, and shared values.

Intuitive Parenting:

Raj and Priya practiced open communication and active listening with their children. They encouraged Aarav and Ananya to express their feelings and concerns, fostering a sense of trust and understanding.

Flip Side: Without intuitive parenting, children might feel misunderstood and insecure, affecting their emotional development.

Key Takeaway: Intuitive parenting strengthens the parent-child bond and promotes emotional intelligence.

Acts of Kindness:

The Sharma's engaged in random acts of kindness, like helping a neighbour or feeding stray animals. These acts instilled the value of kindness and compassion in their children.

Flip Side: Without these acts, the children might lack a sense of interconnectedness and shared responsibility for others' well-being.

Key Takeaway: Acts of kindness foster a sense of interconnectedness and shared responsibility.

Mindful Eating:

During meals, the Sharma's practiced mindful eating, paying attention to Flavors, textures, and the act of nourishing their bodies. This emphasized the sacredness of daily rituals and connected spirituality to everyday life.

Flip Side: Without mindful eating, the family might miss the opportunity to appreciate and Savor their meals, leading to a disconnect from the act of nourishment.

Key Takeaway: Mindful eating emphasizes the sacredness of daily rituals and fosters a connection between spirituality and everyday life.

Conclusion:

Through these spiritual practices, the Sharma family nurtured a harmonious and fulfilling life. They discovered that spirituality enriched their relationships, instilled values, and created a sense of purpose and connection. While the flip side highlighted potential gaps, their commitment to spiritual parenting ensured a loving and supportive environment for Aarav and Ananya to thrive.

Key Takeaways:

1. **Mindfulness and Presence:** Enhances connection and presence in shared moments.

2. **Gratitude Practices:** Cultivates a positive mindset and appreciation.

3. **Connection with Nature:** Fosters interconnectedness and environmental stewardship.

4. **Values-Based Storytelling:** Transmits cultural and ethical values.

5. **Mind-Body Practices:** Enhances emotional regulation and inner peace.

6. **Community Engagement:** Fosters empathy, compassion, and responsibility.

7. **Rituals and Traditions:** Establishes continuity, stability, and shared values.

8. **Intuitive Parenting:** Strengthens bonds and promotes emotional intelligence.

9. **Acts of Kindness:** Instills kindness and a sense of interconnectedness.

10. **Mindful Eating:** Connects spirituality to everyday life through appreciation. Role of Spirituality in healthy Parenting Style

Spirituality in the context of parenting refers to a set of values, beliefs, and practices that go beyond the material aspects of life and encompass a sense of purpose, connection, and meaning. Integrating spirituality into healthy parenting can have various benefits for both parents and children. Here are some ways to demonstrate and inculcate spirituality through natural activities and games, along with their advantages:

1. **Mindfulness and Presence:**
- **Activity:** Introduce simple mindfulness exercises like deep breathing, meditation, or guided visualization
- Teach and practice mindfulness through activities like nature walks, where you encourage your child to observe and appreciate the beauty around them.
- **Advantage:** Enhances the parent-child relationship by fostering a deeper connection and presence during shared moments.

2. **Gratitude Practices:**
- **Activity:** Create a family gratitude jar where each member can write down something they are thankful for and share it during family time.
- **Advantage:** Cultivates a positive mindset, teaches appreciation, and reinforces the importance of acknowledging blessings.

3. **Connection with Nature:**
   - **Activity:** Engage in outdoor activities like gardening, camping, or simply star-gazing to instill a sense of wonder and connection with the natural world.
   - **Advantage:** Fosters a sense of interconnectedness, environmental stewardship, and an appreciation for the beauty of the Earth.

4. **Values-Based Storytelling:**
   - **Activity:** Share stories that highlight spiritual and moral values during bedtime or family gatherings.
   - **Advantage:** Helps in transmitting cultural and ethical values, guiding children in making positive choices.

5. **Mind-Body Practices:**
   - **Activity:** Introduce simple yoga or meditation exercises suitable for children to promote a mind-body connection.
   - **Advantage:** Enhances emotional regulation, reduces stress, and instills a sense of inner peace.

6. **Community Engagement:**
   - **Activity:** Volunteer together as a family for community service projects, emphasizing the importance of helping others.
   - **Advantage:** Fosters empathy, compassion, and a sense of responsibility towards the well-being of others.

7. **Rituals and Traditions:**
   - **Activity:** Create family rituals or traditions that hold spiritual significance, such as a weekly family meal or a special ceremony.
   - **Advantage:** Establishes a sense of continuity, stability, and shared values within the family.

8. **Intuitive Parenting:**
- **Activity:** Encourage open communication and active listening between parents and children to foster a sense of trust and understanding.
- **Advantage:** Strengthens the parent-child bond, promotes emotional intelligence, and helps children develop a secure attachment.

9. **Acts of Kindness:**
- **Activity:** Engage in random acts of kindness as a family.
- **Significance:** Instilling the value of kindness and compassion contributes to a sense of interconnectedness and a shared responsibility for the well-being of others.

10. **Mindful Eating:**
- **Activity:** Practice mindful eating during family meals, paying attention to the flavours, textures, and the act of nourishing the body.
- **Significance:** This activity emphasizes the sacredness of daily rituals and fosters a connection between spirituality and the everyday aspects of life.

Advantages of Spirituality in Healthy Parenting:

1. **Emotional Resilience:** Children exposed to spiritual practices tend to develop emotional resilience, coping skills, and a positive outlook on life.

2. **Values and Morality:** Spiritual teachings often provide a moral compass, guiding children to make ethical choices and understand the consequences of their actions.

3. **Sense of Purpose:** Introducing spirituality helps children develop a sense of purpose and meaning, contributing to their overall well-being.

4. **Family Cohesion:** Spiritual activities strengthen family bonds by creating shared experiences and values that promote a sense of belonging.

5. **Stress Reduction:** Spiritual practices like mindfulness and meditation can be effective tools for managing stress, both for parents and children.

6. **Healthy Relationships:** Emphasizing values such as love, compassion, and empathy contributes to the development of healthy, respectful relationships.

7. **Personal Growth:** Integrating spirituality encourages self-reflection, personal growth, and a deeper understanding of oneself and others.

By incorporating these natural activities and games into parenting, you can create a nurturing environment that promotes spiritual values, fostering the holistic development of your child.

Peer Pressure and Influences in Parenting

Story: Resisting Peer Pressure: Aesika's Journey

Story:

In a bustling town in India, nestled between ancient temples and modern malls, lived a bright 12-year-old girl named Aesika. She loved nature and often spent her weekends hiking with her father, Raj. Aesika was popular in school, but as she transitioned to middle school, she began to feel the pressures of fitting in.

One day, Aesika came home looking troubled. Raj noticed and decided it was time for a heart-to-heart conversation during their usual evening walk in the nearby park. They watched the sunset while Aesika shared her concerns about wanting to fit in with her new classmates. Some of them had started bringing expensive gadgets to school and flaunting branded clothes, making Aesika feel left out.

Understanding the importance of addressing peer pressure, Raj decided to use their time in nature to teach Aesika some valuable lessons. The next day, they watched an age-appropriate movie that highlighted the impact of peer pressure. Afterward, they discussed the characters' choices and how media can shape perceptions. This helped Aesika develop critical thinking skills and understand the media's influence on her and her friends.

Raj also organized a playdate with Aesika's classmates and their parents. They spent the day playing traditional Indian games like kho-kho and kabaddi, building strong connections and promoting a healthy social environment. Aesika felt more at ease knowing her friends' parents and recognizing that they shared similar values.

To tackle the influence of social media, Raj and Aesika set guidelines for safe and responsible use. They agreed on specific times for social media and focused on using it positively. This fostered digital literacy and promoted a healthy relationship with technology.

Raj encouraged Aesika to pursue her individual interests. She loved painting, so he enrolled her in a local art class. Aesika found joy in expressing herself through art, which boosted her self-worth and provided a fulfilling escape from peer pressure.

One weekend, Raj introduced mindfulness and relaxation techniques during their nature hikes. They practiced deep breathing exercises while sitting by the river, helping Aesika manage stress and anxiety. This promoted emotional intelligence and self-awareness, enabling her to make thoughtful decisions.

Raj also engaged Aesika in role-playing scenarios involving peer pressure. They acted out situations where she had to assert herself against negative influences. This built her confidence and equipped her with practical skills to handle challenging situations.

Understanding the importance of positive peer relationships, Raj encouraged Aesika to form friendships with supportive classmates. He arranged group activities that fostered teamwork and camaraderie, reinforcing healthy behaviours and providing a strong support network.

Finally, Raj and Aesika set realistic expectations together. They established achievable goals, emphasizing the importance of self-acceptance and personal growth. This reduced the likelihood of succumbing to unrealistic societal pressures and promoted a sense of accomplishment.

Key Takeaways:

1. **Open Communication:** Create a safe space for children to express themselves without judgment. Regular family discussions build trust and strengthen the parent-child bond, addressing peer pressure proactively.

2. **Identifying Values:** Jointly establish family values to provide a foundation for decision-making. This helps children develop a strong sense of self and resist negative influences.

3. **Role-Playing Scenarios:** Practice assertiveness and decision-making through role-playing. This builds confidence and equips children with practical skills to handle peer pressure.

4. **Encourage Individual Interests:** Support and encourage children's hobbies to foster a sense of identity and self-worth outside of peer influence. This enhances resilience and provides fulfilment.

5. **Mindfulness and Emotional Regulation:** Introduce mindfulness techniques to help children manage stress and anxiety. This promotes emotional intelligence and thoughtful decision-making.

6. **Teach Critical Thinking:** Engage in discussions that encourage critical thinking and problem-solving. This develops children's ability to analyse situations and make independent decisions.

7. **Positive Peer Relationships:** Encourage forming positive friendships to strengthen resilience to negative peer pressure. A supportive network reinforces healthy behaviours.

8. **Set Realistic Expectations:** Establish achievable goals to reduce the impact of societal pressures. This promotes self-acceptance and diminishes the influence of external factors.

By incorporating these strategies, parents can help their children navigate peer pressure in a healthy and constructive manner, fostering resilience and individuality in their personal growth journey.

Peer Pressure and Influences in Parenting:

Peer pressure refers to the influence exerted by a person's peers, or social group, in order to encourage them to change their attitudes, behaviours, or values to conform to those of the influencing group. In the context of parenting, peer pressure can indirectly affect children through their interactions with friends, classmates, or other individuals in their social circles. It can influence their choices, behaviours, and attitudes.

In the process of healthy parenting, understanding and addressing peer pressure is crucial. Nature-based activities and games can be valuable tools to help children cope with peer pressure, fostering resilience and individuality.

1. **Media Influence:**
- **Activity:** Watch age-appropriate movies or TV shows together, and discuss the content.
- **Advantages:** Helps children develop critical thinking skills and understand media influence.

2. **School and Friends:**
- **Activity:** Encourage playdates and get to know your child's friends and their parents.

- **Advantages:** Building strong connections with your child's social circle can provide insights and facilitate open communication.

3. **Social Media:**
- **Activity:** Establish guidelines for safe and responsible social media use.
- **Advantages:** Fosters digital literacy and promotes a healthy relationship with technology.

4. **Educational Influences:**
- **Activity:** Engage in educational games or activities that align with your child's interests.
- **Advantages:** Helps channel external influences into positive learning experiences.

Coping with peer pressure and external influences is a common concern for parents. Incorporating activities-based techniques into your parenting approach can be an effective way to foster a healthy and resilient mindset in your child. Here are some strategies, their significance, and the advantages associated with them:

1. Open Communication:
- **Activity:** Engage in regular family discussions or activities that encourage open communication.
- **Significance:** Create a safe space for your child to express themselves without judgment.
- **Advantages:** Helps build trust, strengthens the parent-child bond, and allows you to address peer pressure issues proactively.

2. Identifying Values:
- **Activity:** Jointly establish family values and discuss their importance.
- **Significance:** Provides a foundation for decision-making and helps your child develop a strong sense of self.

- **Advantages:** Gives your child a clear framework to resist negative influences and make informed choices.

3. Role-Playing Scenarios:

- **Activity:** Role-play different scenarios involving peer pressure.
- **Significance:** Helps your child practice assertiveness and decision-making in a safe environment.
- **Advantages:** Builds confidence and equips them with practical skills to handle challenging situations.

4. Encourage Individual Interests:

- **Activity:** Support and encourage your child's individual interests and hobbies.
- **Significance:** Fosters a sense of identity and self-worth outside of peer influence.
- **Advantages:** Enhances resilience and provides a source of fulfillment that may reduce the impact of peer pressure.

5. Mindfulness and Emotional Regulation:

- **Activity:** Introduce mindfulness and relaxation techniques.
- **Significance:** Helps your child manage stress, anxiety, and peer pressure more effectively.
- **Advantages:** Promotes emotional intelligence, self-awareness, and the ability to make thoughtful decisions.

6. Teach Critical Thinking:

- **Activity:** Engage in discussions that encourage critical thinking and problem-solving.
- **Significance:** Develops your child's ability to analyze situations and make decisions based on their values.
- **Advantages:** Equips them with the skills to navigate peer pressure with a thoughtful and independent mindset.

7. Positive Peer Relationships:

- **Activity:** Encourage your child to form positive friendships.
- **Significance:** Surrounding your child with positive influences strengthens their resilience to negative peer pressure.
- **Advantages:** Fosters a supportive network and reinforces healthy behaviors.

8. Set Realistic Expectations:

- **Activity:** Establish achievable goals and expectations with your child.
- **Significance:** Reduces the likelihood of succumbing to unrealistic societal pressures.
- **Advantages:** Promotes a sense of accomplishment and self-acceptance, diminishing the impact of external influences.

By incorporating these activities into your parenting routine, you can help your child develop the skills and mindset needed to navigate peer pressure in a healthy and constructive manner. It's crucial to maintain open communication, provide guidance, and foster a supportive environment that encourages individuality and positive decision-making.

Allow our Children to Fail: As Failure is One of Biggest Teacher in Life

The Tale of Ishan and His Adventures in Nature

Story

In a small village in India, there lived a young boy named Ishan. He was curious, energetic, and always eager to explore the world around him. Ishan's parents, Priya and Ravi, believed in the importance of letting him experience the world, including its failures and setbacks, to help him grow resilient and capable.

One summer, Priya and Ravi decided to take Ishan on a series of nature-based adventures to teach him valuable life lessons. Their first adventure was a Nature Scavenger Hunt. Ishan was excited to find various items like unique leaves, colourful stones, and flowers. Despite his enthusiasm, he couldn't find all the items on the list. Feeling disheartened, he looked up at his parents. Ravi gently explained, "Not every attempt is successful, Ishan. What's important is that you enjoyed the hunt and learned from the experience. Persistence is key."

Next, they embarked on building a Miniature Shelter in the nearby forest. Using sticks, leaves, and twigs, Ishan constructed a small hut. However, a sudden gust of wind toppled his creation. Priya smiled and said, "It's okay, Ishan. Let's figure out what went wrong and try again. This is how we learn and become better problem solvers."

For their third adventure, Ishan gathered pinecones, pebbles, and leaves to create Nature Art. When his artwork didn't turn out as he imagined, Priya encouraged him, "Mistakes can lead to unique and beautiful outcomes. Creativity often blossoms from unexpected results."

In their garden, Ishan planted seeds and eagerly waited for them to grow. Despite his efforts, some plants didn't thrive. Priya explained, "Not all plants grow as we hope, Ishan. This teaches us about the needs of living things and resilience. We learn from our mistakes and try again."

Ishan also started Nature Journaling, recording his observations about the environment. Some days, he missed entries or struggled with his drawings. Ravi reminded him, "Improvement comes with practice. Consistency and patience are important."

They joined a local conservation project, cleaning up a nearby river. Despite their best efforts, the river wasn't completely clean. Ravi pointed out, "Environmental issues are complex. We must learn from setbacks and think critically about how to improve our efforts."

For a Teamwork and Collaboration activity, Ishan and his friends built a birdhouse. They faced challenges in coordination, but they learned the importance of working together to achieve common goals.

Observing the natural processes around them, Ishan saw that not all eggs hatched and not all seeds germinated. Priya explained, "Failure is a natural part of life. Understanding this helps us appreciate the cycles of nature."

On a nature hike, Ishan had to make decisions with minimal guidance. He sometimes chose the wrong path, but each mistake helped him develop better risk assessment skills and critical thinking.

During a camping trip, they faced sudden rain. Ishan learned to regulate his emotions and adapt to unexpected changes, managing frustration and maintaining composure.

Key Takeaways

1. **Resilience Building:** Experiencing failure in a supportive environment helps build resilience, teaching children that setbacks are a natural part of life and can be overcome.

2. **Problem-Solving Skills:** Failure provides opportunities for problem-solving, guiding children to analyse what went wrong and find solutions.

3. **Learning from Mistakes:** Embracing failure fosters a growth mindset, encouraging curiosity and the willingness to try again.

4. **Building Confidence:** Successfully navigating through failure boosts a child's confidence and self-efficacy.

5. **Adaptability:** Experiencing setbacks in nature-based activities teaches children to be flexible and open to new approaches.

6. **Environmental Awareness:** Understanding the complexities of environmental issues through failure encourages critical thinking and better efforts in conservation.

7. **Teamwork and Collaboration:** Failures in coordination and communication highlight the importance of teamwork and shared responsibility.

8. **Understanding Natural Processes:** Observing natural failures helps children grasp the unpredictability and variability of life.

9. **Risk Assessment and Decision-Making:** Experiencing failures in judgment fosters the development of risk assessment skills and critical thinking.

10. **Emotional Regulation:** Facing unexpected challenges in nature teaches children to regulate their emotions and adapt to unforeseen circumstances.

By allowing Ishan to experience failures through these nature-based activities, Priya and Ravi equipped him with essential life skills, making him resilient, adaptable, and confident in navigating the world around him.

Allow our children to Fail: As Failure is one of biggest teacher in life:

Failure plays a crucial role in the process of parenting as it fosters resilience, growth, and skill development in children. Incorporating nature-based activities into parenting provides an excellent context for experiencing and learning from failures.

Nature-based activities and games not only provide enjoyable experiences for children but also offer valuable opportunities for learning and development. Incorporating the concept of failure in these activities can contribute to essential life skills and resilience. Here are some nature-based activities along with the importance of embracing failure in the parenting process:

1. **Nature Scavenger Hunt:**
- **Activity:** Create a list of items for your child to find in a natural setting, such as leaves, rocks, or flowers.
- **Importance of Failure:** If your child doesn't find all the items, it teaches them that not every attempt is successful. Emphasize the importance of persistence and learning from the experience.
- **Resilience Building:**
- Allowing children to experience failure in a supportive environment helps build resilience. It teaches them that setbacks are a natural part of life and that they can overcome challenges.

2. **Building a Miniature Shelter:**
   - **Activity:** Use natural materials like sticks, leaves, and twigs to construct a small shelter in your backyard or a park.
   - **Importance of Failure:** If the shelter falls apart, it's an opportunity to discuss what went wrong, problem-solving, and trying again. This teaches resilience and adaptability.
   - **Problem-Solving Skills:**
   - Failure provides opportunities for problem-solving. Parents can guide children in analysing what went wrong, identifying solutions, and implementing changes in their approach.

3. **Nature Art:**
   - **Activity:** Collect various natural materials like pinecones, pebbles, and leaves to create artwork outdoors.
   - **Importance of Failure:** If the art doesn't turn out as expected, it encourages creativity, adaptability, and the understanding that mistakes can lead to unique and beautiful outcomes.
   - **Learning from Mistakes:**
   - Embracing failure fosters a growth mindset, where children understand that mistakes are opportunities for learning. It encourages curiosity and a willingness to try again.

4. **Planting and Gardening:**
   - **Activity:** Involve your child in planting seeds, caring for plants, and watching them grow.
   - **Importance of Failure:** If a plant doesn't thrive, it's a lesson in understanding the needs of living things, resilience, and the importance of learning from mistakes for future success.
   - **Building Confidence:**
   - Successfully navigating through failure boosts a child's confidence. Knowing they can overcome obstacles instils a sense of self-efficacy and belief in their abilities.

5. **Nature Journaling:**
- **Activity:** Encourage your child to keep a nature journal where they can sketch, write, or record observations about the environment.
- **Importance of Failure:** If they miss a day or struggle with drawing, it teaches consistency, patience, and the idea that improvement comes with practice.
- **Adaptability:**
- Nature is unpredictable, and failure is a part of adapting to changing circumstances. Experiencing setbacks in nature-based activities teaches children to be flexible and open to new approaches.

6. **Environmental Awareness:**
- **Nature-based Activity:** Participating in a conservation or cleanup project.
- **Advantage:** Even with the best intentions, not every environmental initiative will achieve the desired outcome. This failure teaches children the complexities of environmental issues and encourages them to think critically about how to address and learn from setbacks in conservation efforts.

7. **Teamwork and Collaboration:**
- **Nature-based Activity:** Building a birdhouse or constructing a bird feeder.
- **Advantage:** Children working together may face challenges in creating a functional birdhouse. Failures in coordination and communication provide opportunities for them to understand the importance of teamwork, collaboration, and shared responsibility in achieving common goals.

8. **Understanding Natural Processes:**
- **Nature-based Activity:** Observing the life cycle of plants or animals in a natural setting.

- **Advantage:** Not all eggs hatch, and not all seeds germinate. Experiencing these natural processes helps children grasp the concept of unpredictability and variability in life. It teaches them that failure is a normal part of the cycle and contributes to a deeper understanding of the natural world.

9. **Risk Assessment and Decision-Making:**
- **Nature-based Activity:** Going on a nature hike with minimal guidance.
- **Advantage:** Children might encounter situations where they make incorrect decisions, such as choosing the wrong path. Experiencing failures in judgment fosters the development of risk assessment skills, critical thinking, and the ability to make informed decisions in unfamiliar situations.

10. **Emotional Regulation:**
- **Nature-based Activity:** Encountering adverse weather conditions during a camping trip.
- **Advantage:** Facing unexpected challenges in nature, like sudden rain or a change in weather, helps children regulate their emotions. They learn to adapt to unforeseen circumstances, manage frustration, and maintain composure in the face of adversity.

In summary, failure in the context of nature-based activities provides valuable life lessons for children, contributing to their emotional, intellectual, and social development. It helps them become resilient, resourceful problem solvers who are better equipped to navigate the complexities of the world around them.

Parenting Excursion with Chanakya

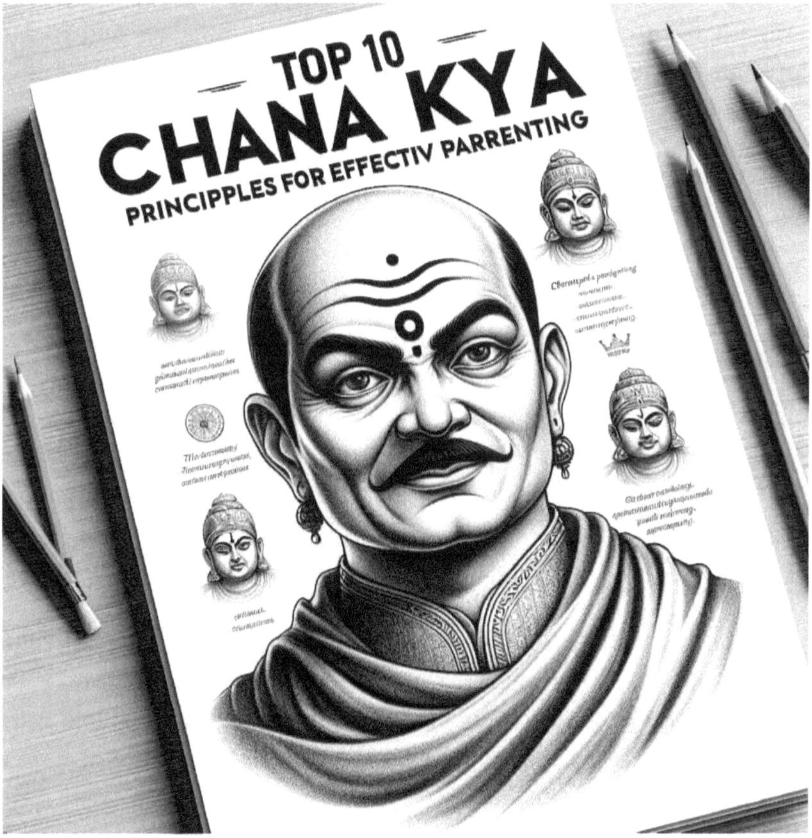

Parenting with Chanakya: An Inspirational Story

Introduction: In a quaint village in India, lived a couple, Raj and Meera, who were blessed with a beautiful baby boy named Aarav. Raj, a school teacher, and Meera, a homemaker, were devoted parents who sought to raise their son with the best values and principles. One day, while cleaning the attic, Raj found an old book titled "Arthashastra" by Chanakya. Intrigued, he began reading it and discovered Chanakya's profound wisdom on various aspects of life, including parenting.

Inspired, Raj and Meera decided to follow Chanakya's teachings to nurture Aarav through different stages of his life.

Infancy (0-2 years): Principle: Provide unconditional love and care, nourishment, and security.

Raj and Meera ensured Aarav's basic needs were always met. They created a warm and loving environment, singing lullabies and rocking him gently to sleep. Whenever Aarav cried, Meera would hold him close, comforting him with her presence. The bond they formed during these early years laid a strong foundation of trust and security for Aarav.

Toddlerhood (2-5 years): Principle: Foster exploration and learning through play.

As Aarav grew into a curious toddler, Raj and Meera encouraged his exploration and learning. They provided him with age-appropriate toys and engaged him in activities that stimulated his creativity and motor skills. One afternoon, Raj sat with Aarav, building towers with colourful blocks. Aarav's eyes sparkled with joy as he stacked the blocks higher, and Raj gently guided him, teaching him patience and perseverance.

Early Childhood (6-10 years): Principle: Instil values and discipline through stories and examples.

When Aarav turned six, Raj and Meera began to teach him moral values through stories. Every night, Raj would narrate tales of brave and virtuous figures from history and mythology. One evening, he told Aarav the story of King Harishchandra, who stood by his principles of honesty and integrity despite immense hardships. Inspired by these stories, Aarav started exhibiting honesty and kindness in his daily interactions.

Pre-Adolescence (11-13 years): Principle: Foster open communication and trust.

As Aarav entered pre-adolescence, Raj and Meera focused on maintaining open communication. They scheduled regular one-on-one time with him, where they discussed his school, friends, and any challenges he faced. During one of these sessions, Aarav confided in Meera about a bully at school. Meera listened patiently, offered advice, and together, they devised a plan to handle the situation. This openness strengthened the trust between them.

Adolescence (14-18 years): Principle: Encourage autonomy while providing support and guidance.

In his teenage years, Aarav sought more independence. Raj and Meera respected his growing autonomy but remained involved in his life. They allowed him to make decisions, like choosing extracurricular activities and managing his schedule, while being there for guidance. Aarav decided to join the school's robotics club, and Raj supported him by helping with projects and attending competitions. This balance of independence and support helped Aarav develop confidence and responsibility.

Young Adulthood (18+ years): Principle: Transition to a mentorship role while respecting their autonomy.

As Aarav stepped into young adulthood, Raj and Meera transitioned to a mentorship role. They encouraged him to pursue his dreams and take responsibility for his choices. When Aarav sought advice on career choices, Raj shared his insights but respected Aarav's decision to follow his passion for engineering. Meera taught him financial management, guiding him on budgeting and savings while allowing him to learn from his experiences.

Conclusion: By following Chanakya's timeless wisdom, Raj and Meera nurtured Aarav's physical, emotional, and moral growth at each stage of his development. Aarav grew up to be a responsible, confident, and kind-hearted young man, embodying the values his parents had instilled in him. The teachings of Chanakya, though ancient, proved to be a guiding light in modern parenting, shaping Aarav into a well-rounded individual ready to face the world with integrity and wisdom.

Key Takeaways:

1. **Infancy:** Provide unconditional love and security.

2. **Toddlerhood:** Encourage exploration and learning through play.

3. **Early Childhood:** Instill values and discipline through stories.

4. **Pre-Adolescence:** Maintain open communication and trust.

5. **Adolescence:** Encourage autonomy with support and guidance.

6. **Young Adulthood:** Transition to mentorship while respecting autonomy.

This story of Raj, Meera, and Aarav exemplifies the profound impact of Chanakya's teachings on parenting, demonstrating how ancient wisdom can be applied to modern life to nurture well-rounded and virtuous individuals.

Parenting with Chanakya:

Chanakya, also known as Kautilya or Vishnugupta, was an ancient Indian teacher, philosopher, economist, jurist, and royal advisor. He is traditionally identified as the author of the Arthashastra, a treatise on politics, economics, and military strategy.

Chanakya's teachings on parenting emphasize the importance of understanding and adapting to the different stages of a child's development. Here's a breakdown of his approach to upbringing children at various age groups, along with tips and illustrative examples for each stage:

1. **Infancy (0-2 years):**
- Principle: Provide unconditional love and care, nourishment and security.
- Tips: Ensure the child's basic needs are met, including feeding, warmth, and comfort. Create a safe and loving environment.
- Example: Sing lullabies to your infant while rocking them gently to sleep. Respond promptly to their cries to reassure them of your presence.

2. **Toddlerhood (2-5 years):**
- Principle: Foster exploration and learning through play.

- Tips: Encourage curiosity and independence by providing age-appropriate toys and activities. Set clear boundaries and offer gentle guidance.
- Example: Engage in simple games like building blocks or playing with toys that encourage creativity and motor skills development.

3. **Early Childhood (6-10 years):**
- **Principle:** Instil values and discipline through stories and examples.
- **Tips:** Teach moral values through stories, fables, and real-life examples. Encourage honesty, kindness, and responsibility.
- **Example:** Share stories of brave and virtuous figures from history or literature to inspire good character traits in your child.

4. **Pre-Adolescence (11-13 years):**
- **Principle:** Foster open communication and trust.
- **Tips:** Maintain an open dialogue with your child, actively listen to their thoughts and concerns, and offer guidance without judgment.
- **Example:** Schedule regular one-on-one time with your child to discuss school, friends, and any challenges they may be facing.

5. **Adolescence (14-18 years):**
- **Principle:** Encourage autonomy while providing support and guidance.
- **Tips:** Respect your teenager's growing independence while remaining involved in their lives. Set realistic expectations and offer support as they navigate complex emotions and decisions.
- **Example:** Allow your teenager to make some decisions on their own, such as choosing extracurricular activities or managing their own schedule, while providing guidance when needed.

6. **Young Adulthood (18+ years):**
- **Principle:** Transition to a mentorship role while respecting their autonomy.

- **Tips:** Support your young adult in pursuing their goals and dreams, while also encouraging them to take responsibility for their choices and actions.

- **Example:** Offer guidance on important life decisions such as career choices or financial management, while allowing them the freedom to learn from their experiences.

By applying these principles at each stage of a child's development, parents can effectively nurture their children's physical, emotional, and moral growth, following the timeless wisdom of Chanakya.

Title: "Raising Rohan: Chanakya's Wisdom in Modern Parenting"

Part 1: The Importance of Discipline

Rohan was a lively ten-year-old with boundless energy, often bouncing from one activity to another. His parents, Priya and Raj, were determined to instil discipline in him without stifling his exuberance. Inspired by Chanakya's teachings, they decided to introduce a structured routine involving nature-based activities.

Every Sunday, the family would go hiking in the nearby forest. These hikes were not just about physical exercise; they became a cornerstone for teaching Rohan the importance of routine and responsibility. Each family member had a role—Rohan's was to pack snacks and ensure they left on time. As weeks passed, Rohan began to take pride in his responsibilities, realizing the importance of discipline in achieving goals.

Modern Parenting Tip: Priya and Raj set clear rules and routines, consistently reinforcing them with positive reinforcement. Rohan's adherence to his hiking responsibilities was celebrated with praise and occasional treats.

Part 2: The Value of Education

Priya and Raj believed in Chanakya's principle that education is the foundation of a prosperous life. They wanted Rohan to learn beyond the confines of traditional schooling. To do this, they organized educational nature walks, teaching Rohan about the flora, fauna, and the ecosystem.

One Saturday, they ventured into the forest with a field guide. Rohan's eyes sparkled with curiosity as he identified different plants and insects. He even started a nature journal, drawing and writing about his discoveries. This hands-on learning made education exciting and tangible for him.

Modern Parenting Tip: They encouraged curiosity and learning through diverse experiences, fostering a love for reading and exploration in Rohan.

Part 3: Self-Reliance

Chanakya emphasized the importance of self-reliance. Priya and Raj wanted Rohan to grow into an independent thinker and problem-solver. They decided to involve him in building a birdhouse in their backyard.

Rohan was excited about the project. His parents provided the tools and guidance, but it was Rohan who took the lead. He measured, cut, and assembled the pieces, encountering and overcoming several challenges along the way. The pride he felt in completing the birdhouse was immeasurable, boosting his confidence and self-reliance.

Modern Parenting Tip: Priya and Raj encouraged Rohan to tackle age-appropriate tasks independently, guiding him to find solutions rather than providing direct answers.

Part 4: Understanding the Value of Money

Understanding the value of resources was another key lesson from Chanakya. Priya and Raj started a small vegetable garden with Rohan, teaching him the effort required to grow food and the importance of not wasting resources.

Rohan learned to plant seeds, water the plants, and patiently wait for them to grow. He understood the value of each vegetable they harvested, realizing the effort behind it. This experience translated into a newfound respect for money and resources.

Modern Parenting Tip: They taught Rohan about saving and budgeting through allowances, setting savings goals for items he wished to purchase.

Part 5: Ethical Living

Ethical living was a principle Chanakya held dear. Priya and Raj participated in community clean-up drives and wildlife conservation projects, involving Rohan in these activities to instil a sense of responsibility towards the environment and community.

One memorable day, the family joined a beach clean-up drive. Rohan's small hands picked up trash, and he understood the impact of his actions on the environment. This experience planted seeds of ethical living and community responsibility in his young mind.

Modern Parenting Tip: Priya and Raj led by example, demonstrating honesty, kindness, and respect in their daily actions and interactions.

Part 6: Respect for Nature

Living in harmony with nature was a core principle for Chanakya. Priya and Raj took Rohan on regular family camping trips, immersing him in natural settings and teaching him to appreciate and care for the environment.

During one camping trip, Rohan watched a sunrise over the mountains. The beauty of nature left a profound impact on him, fostering a deep respect for all living beings. He learned to leave no trace, understanding his role in protecting the environment.

Modern Parenting Tip: They encouraged eco-friendly practices at home, such as recycling, conserving water, and reducing waste.

Part 7: Patience and Perseverance

Chanakya taught that success comes to those who are patient and persist in their efforts. Raj introduced Rohan to bird watching, an activity requiring immense patience.

Rohan spent hours in the backyard, waiting quietly for birds to visit the feeder. His patience was rewarded when he spotted a rare bird one afternoon. This experience taught him that patience and perseverance lead to success, a lesson that extended to his studies and other activities.

Modern Parenting Tip: They encouraged Rohan to take on challenging tasks, supporting him through his struggles and emphasizing the value of persistence.

Part 8: Effective Communication

Clear and thoughtful communication was key to Chanakya's teachings. Priya and Raj organized family hiking trips where they could talk and share thoughts without the distractions of technology.

One evening, during a hike, Rohan opened up about a problem he was facing at school. The family discussed it openly, finding a solution together. These hikes became a safe space for Rohan to express his feelings, strengthening family bonds through effective communication.

Modern Parenting Tip: They fostered an environment where open and honest communication was encouraged, ensuring everyone felt heard.

Part 9: Leadership and Responsibility

Chanakya emphasized leadership and responsibility. Priya and Raj allowed Rohan to plan and lead a family picnic in the park.

Rohan organized the event meticulously, from deciding the menu to planning games. He learned to take responsibility and guide others, developing his leadership and organizational skills. The picnic was a success, and Rohan's confidence soared.

Modern Parenting Tip: They encouraged Rohan to take on leadership roles in small family projects, providing guidance and support as needed.

Part 10: Adaptability

Adaptability was crucial for success, according to Chanakya. Priya and Raj enrolled Rohan in an outdoor survival skills workshop, teaching him to adapt to different situations.

Rohan learned to build shelters, start fires, and find food in the wild. These skills not only made him adaptable but also boosted his problem-solving abilities and resilience.

Modern Parenting Tip: They encouraged problem-solving and creative thinking by presenting Rohan with various scenarios and challenges to overcome, highlighting the importance of adaptability.

Conclusion

Through these nature-based activities and modern parenting tips, Priya and Raj successfully integrated Chanakya's wisdom into their parenting approach. Rohan grew up to be disciplined, educated, self-reliant, and ethical, with a deep respect for nature and the values of patience, effective communication, leadership, and adaptability.

The principles derived from Chanakya's wisdom, coupled with modern parenting techniques, not only equipped Rohan with essential life skills but also fostered a profound connection with the environment, promoting a holistic approach to parenting in the modern world.

Key Takeaways

1. **Discipline:** Establish clear routines and responsibilities through engaging activities.

2. **Education:** Foster curiosity and learning beyond traditional schooling.

3. **Self-Reliance:** Encourage independence and problem-solving skills.

4. **Value of Money:** Teach the value of resources through hands-on experiences.

5. **Ethical Living:** Instill community responsibility and ethical behavior.

6. **Respect for Nature:** Promote eco-friendly practices and a love for the environment.

7. **Patience and Perseverance:** Emphasize the importance of persistence.

8. **Effective Communication:** Create spaces for open and honest communication.

9. **Leadership and Responsibility:** Provide opportunities for leadership and responsibility.

10. **Adaptability:** Encourage adaptability through diverse challenges and scenarios.

Principles derived from Chanakya's Wisdom

Here are principles derived from Chanakya's wisdom that can be applied to effective and healthy parenting, along with nature-based activities and modern parenting tips to achieve these principles:

1. **Importance of Discipline:**
- **Chanakya Principle:** Discipline is crucial for success and should be instilled from a young age.
- **Nature-Based Activity:** Engage in regular outdoor activities like hiking or gardening at specific times to instil a sense of routine and responsibility.
- **Modern Parenting Tip:** Set clear rules and routines for your children and be consistent with them. Use positive reinforcement to encourage adherence to these routines.

2. **Value of Education:**
- **Chanakya Principle:** Education is the foundation of a prosperous life.
- **Nature-Based Activity:** Organize educational nature walks to teach children about flora, fauna, and the ecosystem, emphasizing learning through exploration.
- **Modern Parenting Tip:** Encourage curiosity and learning, not just through traditional schooling but through diverse experiences and reading.

3. **Self-Reliance:**
- **Chanakya Principle:** Being self-reliant and independent is essential for personal growth.
- **Nature-Based Activity:** Involve children in building simple outdoor structures like birdhouses, fostering creativity and problem-solving skills.
- **Modern Parenting Tip:** Encourage children to take on age-appropriate tasks independently, guiding them to find solutions rather than providing direct answers.

4. **Understanding the Value of Money:**
- **Chanakya Principle:** One must understand the value of resources and use them wisely.
- **Nature-Based Activity:** Start a small vegetable garden, teaching children the effort required to grow food and the importance of not wasting resources.
- **Modern Parenting Tip:** Teach children about saving and budgeting through allowances and savings goals for items they wish to purchase.

5. **Ethical Living:**
- **Chanakya Principle:** Ethics and morals form the cornerstone of a virtuous life.
- **Nature-Based Activity:** Participate in community clean-up drives or wildlife conservation projects to instil a sense of responsibility towards the environment and community.
- **Modern Parenting Tip:** Lead by example, demonstrating honesty, kindness, and respect in your daily actions and interactions.

6. **Respect for Nature:**
- **Chanakya Principle:** One should live in harmony with nature and respect all living beings.

- **Nature-Based Activity:** Regular family camping trips or nature retreats to immerse children in natural settings, teaching them to appreciate and care for the environment.
- **Modern Parenting Tip:** Encourage eco-friendly practices at home like recycling, conserving water, and reducing waste.

7. **Patience and Perseverance:**
- **Chanakya Principle:** Success comes to those who are patient and persist in their efforts.
- **Nature-Based Activity:** Engage in activities like bird watching or planting trees, which require patience and time to see results.
- **Modern Parenting Tip:** Encourage children to take on challenging tasks and support them through their struggles, emphasizing the value of persistence.

8. **Effective Communication:**
- **Chanakya Principle:** Clear and thoughtful communication is key to resolving conflicts and building relationships.
- **Nature-Based Activity:** Organize family hiking or walking trips where family members can talk and share thoughts without the distractions of technology.
- **Modern Parenting Tip:** Foster an environment where open and honest communication is encouraged, and everyone feels heard.

9. **Leadership and Responsibility:**
- **Chanakya Principle:** Leadership is about taking responsibility and guiding others towards a common goal.
- **Nature-Based Activity:** Allow children to plan and lead a family outdoor activity, helping them develop leadership and organizational skills.
- **Modern Parenting Tip:** Encourage children to take on leadership roles in small family projects or group activities, providing guidance and support as needed.

10. Adaptability:

- **Chanakya Principle:** Being adaptable in the face of challenges is crucial for success.

- **Nature-Based Activity:** Engage in outdoor survival skills workshops or camps that teach children how to adapt to different situations.

- **Modern Parenting Tip:** Encourage problem-solving and creative thinking by presenting children with various scenarios and challenges to overcome, highlighting the importance of adaptability.

Implementing these principles through nature-based activities not only helps inculcate valuable life skills in children but also fosters a deep connection with the environment, promoting a holistic approach to parenting in the modern world.

Keeping our Child Safe Online

Story: A Journey of Safe Surfing: Arya's Online Adventure

Introduction

In a small town in India, nestled between lush green fields and winding rivers, lived a curious and bright 10-year-old boy named Arya. Arya loved exploring new things, and lately, he had become fascinated with the internet. His parents, understanding both the opportunities and dangers of the online world, decided to guide Arya on how to navigate the internet safely.

The Beginning

One sunny morning, Arya's father, Mr. Sharma, sat him down for a chat. "Arya, the internet is like a vast ocean. It has many wonderful things, but also some dangers. We need to learn how to swim safely," he began.

Arya's eyes widened with excitement and curiosity. "How do we do that, Papa?"

"Let's start with some simple rules," Mr. Sharma said. They created a family media plan together, deciding on screen-free times, approved websites, and online behaviour guidelines. Arya felt important and involved in making these decisions.

Learning Through Play

To make learning about online safety fun, Arya's parents organized role-playing scenarios. They pretended to be online strangers, teaching Arya how to respond to friend requests and messages from unknown people. Arya practiced saying, "No, thank you," and telling his parents if something made him uncomfortable.

One day, Mrs. Sharma found a website with educational games about cybersecurity. Arya played a game where he had to identify phishing attempts and avoid malware. Each level he completed taught him more about protecting his personal information.

Workshops and Activities

Arya's school organized a Digital Literacy and Safety Workshop. The workshop used interactive games to teach about online risks like cyberbullying and privacy breaches. Arya learned about the importance of strong passwords and the concept of a digital footprint. He even participated in a project creating positive digital content—a video diary about his pet cat, Mittens.

Back home, the Sharma's had a "Tech Day" where they explored privacy settings on Arya's favourite platforms. Arya learned to set strong, memorable passwords using passphrases. His favourite was "MittensLovesFish123!"

The Turning Point

One evening, while Arya was playing an online game, he received a message from a player he didn't know. Remembering what he had learned, Arya didn't respond and showed the message to his parents. They praised him for his quick thinking and reminded him of the importance of talking to an adult if he ever felt unsure.

Mr. Sharma took this opportunity to discuss the permanence of online actions and the digital footprint. They decided to create a blog together, where Arya could share his stories and adventures. This project helped Arya understand the impact of his online presence and the importance of responsible content creation.

Staying Informed and Involved

Arya's parents stayed updated on the latest online trends and potential threats. They made it a habit to explore new websites and online games together, ensuring that Arya was navigating safe online spaces.

They also encouraged Arya to question the credibility of information he found online. During their family discussions, they would analyse social media posts and news articles, teaching Arya the importance of fact-checking and considering the source.

Conclusion

Arya's journey to safe surfing was filled with fun, learning, and family bonding. He learned to navigate the vast ocean of the internet confidently, equipped with knowledge and tools to stay safe.

Key Takeaways

1. **Open Dialogue:** Start conversations about internet safety early and keep them going.

2. **Set Clear Rules:** Establish and involve children in creating rules about online behavior.

3. **Parental Controls:** Use parental controls and monitoring tools to ensure safe browsing.

4. **Educate About Risks:** Teach children about online dangers and the permanence of their actions.

5. **Encourage Critical Thinking:** Instill a habit of questioning and verifying online information.

6. **Promote Positive Behavior:** Model and teach respectful and kind online interactions.

7. **Common Area Usage:** Keep devices in common areas for casual supervision.

8. **Stay Informed:** Regularly update yourself on online trends and threats.

9. **Review Privacy Settings:** Ensure children's profiles are secure and private.

10. **Use Educational Resources:** Utilize tools and games designed to teach online safety.

Keeping our child safe online

Keeping your child safe online involves a combination of education, supervision, and the use of technological tools. Here are some comprehensive steps you can take:

1. Open Dialogue

- Start conversations about internet safety early and keep them going as your child grows.

- Discuss the types of websites that are appropriate and safe for them to visit.

- Educate them about the importance of not sharing personal information online.

2. Set Clear Rules and Expectations

- Establish rules about what is and isn't allowed online and set boundaries on which platforms they can use.
- Set time limits for internet usage to prevent excessive exposure.

3. Use Parental Controls

- Utilize the parental control settings on your internet service, devices, and all digital platforms your child uses. This includes setting up content filters to block inappropriate content.
- Consider using monitoring tools that allow you to see what your child is accessing online without being overly invasive.

4. Educate about Online Risks

- Teach your child about the dangers of the internet, including cyberbullying, predators, and scams.
- Discuss the permanence of online actions and the concept of digital footprint.

5. Encourage Critical Thinking

- Teach your child not to accept friend requests or engage in conversations with strangers online.
- Encourage them to question the credibility of information they find online and to check with an adult if unsure.

6. Promote Positive Online Behavior

- Model positive behavior by being mindful of your own digital footprint and the content you share online.
- Teach them the importance of respect and kindness in online interactions.

7. Keep Computers in Common Areas

- Place computers and devices in common areas of the home to monitor use without being overly intrusive.

- This allows you to casually supervise their online activities.

8. Stay Informed and Involved
- Stay updated on the latest online trends and potential threats.
- Be involved in your child's online world. Ask them to show you their favorite websites and what they like to do online.

9. Review Privacy Settings
- Regularly check privacy settings on social media and gaming platforms to ensure your child's profile is secure.
- Teach your child the importance of keeping accounts private and being cautious about what they share online.

10. Use Educational Resources
- Utilize online safety resources and tools designed for parents and children.
- Many organizations offer guides, videos, and games that educate children about staying safe online in an engaging way.

Remember, the goal is not just to protect your child from the dangers of the internet but also to empower them to navigate the online world safely and responsibly. Regularly revisiting these topics as your child grows and as technology evolves is crucial.

Top of Form

Keeping children safe online is a multifaceted challenge that requires active engagement from parents, educators, and the children themselves. Activity-based techniques can be both educational and fun, helping to instil safe online habits. Here are several measures along with their importance and tips for each:

1. Digital Literacy and Safety Workshops
- **Importance:** These workshops can teach children about online risks such as cyberbullying, privacy breaches, and encountering inappropriate content.

- **Tips:** Use interactive games and scenarios to teach children how to navigate online spaces safely. Resources like Google's "Be Internet Awesome" offer engaging activities for learning about digital safety.

2. Create a Family Media Plan

- **Importance:** Establishing rules and guidelines helps set clear expectations about online behavior and screen time.

- Tips: Involve your child in the creation of the plan to encourage their commitment. The plan could include designated screen-free times, approved apps and websites, and guidelines for online communication.

3. Role-Playing Scenarios

- **Importance:** Role-playing can prepare children for real-world online interactions, teaching them how to respond to situations like cyberbullying or phishing attempts.

- **Tips:** Create scenarios based on age-appropriate potential online issues. Discuss and role-play appropriate responses, emphasizing the importance of telling an adult if they feel uncomfortable.

4. Parent-Child Online Activities

- **Importance:** Engaging in online activities together can provide opportunities for teaching by example, such as practicing positive digital etiquette and demonstrating how to evaluate online content critically.

- **Tips:** Schedule regular times to explore new websites, play online games, or learn new skills together. Use these moments to discuss what makes a website trustworthy or how to treat others respectfully online.

5. Privacy Settings and Security Practices Workshop

- **Importance:** Understanding privacy settings on social media and the importance of strong passwords can protect children from unwanted contact and data breaches.

- **Tips:** Have a "tech day" where you explore privacy settings together on various platforms and devices. Teach children to create strong, memorable passwords using techniques like passphrases.

6. Content Creation Projects

- **Importance:** Creating content can teach children about the permanence of the online world and the impact of their digital footprint.
- **Tips:** Encourage children to create positive digital content, such as a blog, a video diary, or digital art. Discuss the public nature of online postings and the concept of digital footprints.

7. Cybersecurity Games and Apps

- **Importance:** Interactive games designed to teach cybersecurity can make learning about complex topics like malware and phishing engaging and accessible.
- **Tips:** Incorporate educational games that simulate cybersecurity scenarios, teaching children how to protect their devices and personal information in a fun and engaging way.

8. Social Media Literacy Sessions

- **Importance:** Teaching children to critically evaluate the content they see on social media can help them develop a healthy skepticism and reduce the risk of being influenced by misleading information.
- **Tips:** Discuss and analyze different social media posts and news articles to highlight the importance of fact-checking and considering the source of information.

General Tips for All Activities:

- **Engage Regularly:** Make these activities a regular part of your routine to reinforce their importance.
- **Open Communication:** Foster an environment where children feel comfortable sharing their online experiences and concerns.

- **Lead by Example:** Model the online behaviors you want your children to adopt.
- **Stay Informed:** Keep up with the latest in online safety to ensure your advice and strategies are up-to-date.

By integrating these activity-based techniques into your approach to online safety, you can equip children with the knowledge and skills they need to navigate the digital world securely and confidently.

Developing Socialization Skills in Children at Early Stage

Story: "A Journey to the Circle of Friends: Arjun's Story"

Introduction

In the bustling city of Pune, there lived a bright and curious seven-year-old boy named Arjun. Arjun was an only child and loved spending his time reading books and playing video games. While he excelled in his studies, his parents, Anil and Meera, noticed that he struggled with social interactions and often felt lonely. Determined to help Arjun develop better social skills, they decided to enrol him in a unique summer camp that focused on activity-based learning and socialization.

Story

The Camp's First Day: Storytelling Circles

On the first day of camp, Arjun was nervous but excited. The camp began with a storytelling circle, where each child contributed a sentence to build a story. Arjun hesitated at first, but soon found himself enjoying the imaginative process. He learned to listen carefully to his peers and respect their contributions, realizing that his ideas were valued too. This activity helped Arjun enhance his verbal communication and listening skills, setting a positive tone for the rest of the camp.

Role-Playing Games: A Trip to the Zoo

The next activity was a role-playing game where children acted out a trip to the zoo. Arjun was assigned the role of a zookeeper. Through this game, he learned empathy and perspective-taking, understanding the responsibilities and challenges of others. He also enjoyed seeing different perspectives, which broadened his social understanding.

Team Sports: Learning to Work Together

One afternoon, the camp organized a soccer match. Initially hesitant, Arjun soon found joy in playing as part of a team. He learned the importance of teamwork and cooperation, celebrating victories and accepting losses with sportsmanship. This experience significantly boosted his confidence and taught him the value of working towards a common goal.

Crafting Projects: Building a Mural Together

One of Arjun's favourite activities was a group crafting project where they created a large mural. He collaborated with his peers, shared ideas, and worked together to bring their vision to life. This fostered creativity and cooperation, and Arjun felt a sense of accomplishment seeing the mural complete, knowing he had played a crucial part.

Circle Time Discussions: Sharing Thoughts and Feelings

Every day ended with a circle time discussion where children shared their thoughts and feelings. Arjun found a safe space to express himself and learned to actively listen to others. These discussions built his verbal expression and active listening skills, making him more confident in social settings.

Nature Walks and Scavenger Hunts: Discovering Teamwork in Nature

The camp also included nature walks and scavenger hunts. Arjun and his friends explored the outdoors, working in pairs to find hidden items. These activities promoted teamwork and observation skills, encouraging Arjun to collaborate and communicate effectively with his peers.

Buddy Reading Sessions: The Joy of Shared Stories

One rainy afternoon, the children paired up for buddy reading sessions. Arjun enjoyed reading a book with his buddy, taking turns and discussing the story. This not only enhanced his reading skills but also helped him develop empathy and patience.

Group Building Challenges: Constructing with Lego

Building with Lego was another highlight. The children were divided into groups and given themes to construct. Arjun learned the importance of problem-solving and cooperative play. Working together, they created impressive structures, celebrating their collective creativity.

Cooking Projects: Creating Delicious Memories

In the camp's kitchen, Arjun participated in cooking projects. He and his friends made simple snacks, learning to follow instructions and work as a team. The joy of sharing their culinary creations taught Arjun the value of teamwork and the satisfaction of collaborative efforts.

Puppet Shows: Unleashing Imagination

Creating and performing puppet shows allowed Arjun to unleash his imagination. He worked in groups to write stories and make puppets, enhancing his storytelling and verbal communication skills. The laughter and applause from their performances boosted his self-esteem.

Community Service Projects: Giving Back

The camp also engaged in community service projects, like making cards for a local nursing home. Arjun felt a deep sense of empathy and social responsibility, understanding the impact of their efforts on the community.

Dramatic Play Centres: Exploring Social Roles

Dramatic play centres were set up with themes like a grocery store or doctor's office. Arjun enjoyed role-playing different social roles, which fostered empathy and understanding of various professions and social situations.

Emotion Charades: Understanding Feelings

In a fun game of emotion charades, Arjun and his friends acted out different emotions. This helped him recognize and understand various feelings, deepening his emotional vocabulary and empathy.

The Flip Side

Despite these positive experiences, there were challenges. Initially, Arjun found it difficult to adapt to group activities, often feeling overwhelmed. There were moments of disagreement and conflict, especially during team sports and group projects. However, with guidance and support from the camp counsellors, Arjun learned valuable conflict resolution skills and the importance of patience and understanding.

Key Takeaways

1. **Emotional Intelligence:** Arjun learned to understand and express his emotions, as well as empathize with others.

2. **Communication:** His verbal and non-verbal communication skills improved through various activities.

3. **Conflict Resolution:** He developed problem-solving skills and learned to navigate disagreements.

4. **Teamwork and Cooperation:** Group activities taught him the value of working together and supporting each other.

5. **Self-esteem and Confidence:** Positive social interactions boosted his self-esteem and confidence.

Conclusion

By the end of the camp, Arjun had not only made new friends but also developed essential socialization skills. His journey through the camp's activities illustrated the importance of early socialization and the role of activity-based learning in fostering these skills. Arjun returned home with a newfound confidence and a heart full of cherished memories, ready to face the world with his circle of friends.

Developing socialization skills in children at early stage

Developing socialization skills in children at an early stage through activity-based methods can be both effective and enjoyable. Such activities not only engage children but also teach them valuable social skills in a natural, playful context.

Importance of Socialization Skills:

1. **Emotional Intelligence:** Socialization helps children understand their own emotions and those of others, fostering empathy and emotional regulation.

2. **Communication:** Interacting with others enhances verbal and non-verbal communication skills, essential for expressing needs, ideas, and feelings.

3. **Conflict Resolution:** Engaging with peers teaches children how to navigate disagreements and find common ground, promoting problem-solving skills.

4. **Teamwork and Cooperation:** Group activities encourage collaboration, teaching children the value of working together towards a common goal.

5. **Self-esteem and Confidence:** Positive social interactions can boost self-esteem and confidence, helping children feel more secure in various situations.

Developing socialization skills in children through activity-based methods can be both effective and enjoyable. Here are 15 activities and games designed to enhance various social skills in young children, along with the importance and keys to success for each:

1. **Storytelling Circles**
- **Importance:** Enhances verbal communication and listening skills.
- **Activity:** Children sit in a circle and contribute to a collective story, one sentence at a time.
- **Success Key:** Encourage creativity and respect for each child's contribution to build a supportive environment.

2. **Role-Playing Games**
- **Importance:** Teaches empathy and perspective-taking.
- **Activity:** Children act out various roles and scenarios, such as a trip to the grocery store or a day at the zoo.
- **Success Key:** Use diverse scenarios to expose children to different perspectives and social situations.

3. **Team Sports (e.g., Soccer, Basketball)**
- **Importance:** Promotes teamwork, cooperation, and understanding of rules.
- **Activity:** Organize simple team sports that require working together to achieve a goal.
- **Success Key:** Focus on teamwork and sportsmanship rather than competition.

4. **Board Games and Puzzles**
- **Importance:** Encourages turn-taking, patience, and strategic thinking.
- **Activity:** Choose age-appropriate board games and puzzles that require multiple players.
- **Success Key:** Ensure a supportive environment where the focus is on participation and problem-solving.

5. **Music and Dance Activities**
- **Importance:** Enhances non-verbal communication and coordination with others.
- **Activity:** Group music and dance activities where children must synchronize their actions.
- **Success Key:** Use a variety of music and dance styles to encourage expression and cultural appreciation.

6. **Crafting Projects**
- **Importance:** Fosters creativity and collaboration.
- **Activity:** Group crafting projects where children work together to create something, like a mural or a large sculpture.
- **Success Key:** Encourage sharing of ideas and materials to promote cooperation.

7. **Circle Time Discussions**
- **Importance:** Builds verbal expression and active listening skills.
- **Activity:** Daily or weekly circle time where children can share thoughts, feelings, or what they've learned.
- **Success Key:** Ensure each child has a chance to speak and is listened to by the group.

8. **Nature Walks and Scavenger Hunts**
- **Importance:** Promotes teamwork and observation skills.

- **Activity:** Organize guided walks or scavenger hunts in nature, encouraging children to work in pairs or small groups.
- **Success Key:** Use open-ended questions and tasks that encourage discussion and collaboration.

9. **Buddy Reading Sessions**
- **Importance:** Enhances reading and empathy skills.
- **Activity:** Pair up children to read a book together, taking turns reading aloud.
- **Success Key:** Choose books that are appropriate for their reading level and interests to keep them engaged.

10. **Group Building Challenges (e.g., Lego, Blocks)**
- **Importance:** Encourages problem-solving and cooperative play.
- **Activity:** Children work in groups to build a structure based on a theme or challenge.
- **Success Key:** Provide enough materials and encourage each child to contribute to the design and construction.

11. **Cooking Projects**
- **Importance:** Teaches following instructions, teamwork, and the joy of sharing.
- **Activity:** Simple cooking projects where children work together to create a meal or snack.
- **Success Key:** Assign each child a specific task and emphasize the importance of working together for a successful outcome.

12. **Puppet Shows**
- **Importance:** Fosters imagination, storytelling, and verbal communication.
- **Activity:** Children create and perform puppet shows in small groups.

- **Success Key:** Provide a variety of materials for puppet-making and help children brainstorm story ideas.

13. Community Service Projects

- **Importance:** Builds a sense of empathy, community, and social responsibility.
- **Activity:** Engage in simple community service projects, like a neighbourhood clean-up or making cards for a local nursing home.
- **Success Key:** Choose age-appropriate activities and discuss the impact of their efforts on the community.

14. Dramatic Play Centres

- **Importance:** Encourages role-play, empathy, and understanding of social roles.
- **Activity:** Set up thematic play areas, such as a grocery store, doctor's office, or a school, where children can engage in role-play.
- **Success Key:** Rotate themes regularly to expose children to various social roles and settings.

15. Emotion Charades

- **Importance:** Helps children recognize and understand different emotions.
- **Activity:** Children take turns acting out different emotions while others guess what they are.
- **Success Key:** Discuss each emotion afterward to deepen understanding and develop emotional vocabulary.

Incorporating these activities into a child's routine can significantly enhance their social skills. The key to success lies in consistent participation, positive reinforcement, and adapting activities to meet the diverse needs and interests of the children involved.

Nurturing our Child's Potential

Story: The Seeds of Potential

In a small town in India, nestled amidst rolling hills and lush greenery, lived a family named the Sharma's. The Sharma's were a close-knit family of four: Ramesh, the father; Sunita, the mother; and their two children, Priya and Aarav. Ramesh and Sunita believed in the importance of nurturing their children's potential, encouraging them to explore their interests and talents.

Identifying Interests and Talents

One sunny afternoon, Ramesh took Priya and Aarav on a nature walk. As they strolled through the forest, Ramesh noticed Priya's fascination with the different species of birds. She would excitedly point out each bird she saw, asking questions about their colours and songs. Meanwhile, Aarav was captivated by the way the sunlight filtered through the leaves, creating intricate patterns on the forest floor. He began sketching the scenes in his little notebook.

Importance: Early identification of interests can help tailor activities to match, providing a more engaging and fulfilling experience. Success Key: Keep an open mind and avoid projecting your own interests onto your child.

Providing Exposure

To nurture these budding interests, Ramesh and Sunita decided to expose their children to a variety of activities. They enrolled Priya in a birdwatching club and Aarav in an art class. On weekends, they would visit museums, art galleries, and nature reserves. They even introduced them to activities like music, sports, and science experiments.

Importance: Exposure broadens horizons and helps discover hidden passions. Success Key: Offer experiences without pressure or expectations, letting them explore freely.

Listening and Communicating

Sunita made it a point to engage in conversations with Priya and Aarav about their interests. She would ask open-ended questions like, "What do you like most about birdwatching?" and "What inspires your drawings?" This showed the children that their opinions were valued and encouraged them to reflect on their interests.

Importance: Shows that you value their opinions and encourages reflection. Success Key: Actively listen to their responses and validate their feelings, showing genuine interest.

Developing Interests and Talents - Providing Resources

Once Priya and Aarav's interests were identified, Ramesh and Sunita provided the necessary resources. They bought Priya a bird guidebook and a pair of binoculars. For Aarav, they set up a small art studio at home with various drawing materials.

Importance: Access to the right resources accelerates learning and skill development. Success Key: Balance investment with the child's sustained interest to avoid overwhelming them or placing undue financial burden.

Encouraging Practice

They encouraged Priya to spend time birdwatching regularly and Aarav to practice his drawing. They set up a routine that allowed for daily practice, celebrating each small achievement along the way.

Importance: Regular practice is crucial for skill development and mastery. Success Key: Help set realistic goals and celebrate progress to maintain motivation.

Seeking Mentorship

Ramesh found a local ornithologist who mentored Priya, teaching her about bird behaviour and conservation. Aarav's art teacher became his mentor, providing guidance and inspiration.

Importance: Mentors offer expert advice, encouragement, and insights. Success Key: Choose mentors who are skilled and good at communicating with and inspiring young people.

Encouraging Interests and Talents

Celebrating Achievements

The Sharma's celebrated Priya and Aarav's achievements, both big and small. They hosted a small family gathering to showcase Aarav's artwork and took Priya on a special birdwatching trip when she identified a rare species.

Importance: Recognition boosts self-esteem and reinforces the value of efforts. Success Key: Ensure the celebration is proportional to the achievement to avoid creating undue pressure.

Fostering a Growth Mindset

Ramesh and Sunita taught their children that skills and talents can be developed through hard work and learning from mistakes. When Priya struggled to identify a bird or Aarav had a tough day with his drawings, they encouraged them to persevere and view challenges as opportunities to grow.

Importance: Encourages resilience and a positive attitude towards challenges. Success Key: Praise effort and progress rather than innate talent.

Providing Opportunities for Application

They sought real-world opportunities for Priya and Aarav to apply their skills. Priya participated in birdwatching competitions, and Aarav's artwork was displayed at local exhibitions.

Importance: Real-world applications provide valuable experience. Success Key: Choose opportunities appropriate for their skill level to ensure a positive and encouraging experience.

Flip Side: One day, Aarav's interest in art began to wane. He no longer found joy in drawing and seemed disinterested. Sunita noticed and decided to have a heart-to-heart conversation with him. Aarav revealed that he felt overwhelmed by the expectations and pressure to always produce perfect artwork. Sunita reassured him that it was okay to take a break and explore other interests. This conversation relieved Aarav, and he gradually found his way back to art, but this time with a renewed sense of joy and without the pressure.

Key Takeaways

1. **Balance:** Ensure that focusing on interests doesn't lead to an imbalanced lifestyle. Children should have time for free play, relaxation, and socializing.

2. **Adaptability:** Be prepared to shift focus if your child's interests change. It's normal for children to explore various passions.

3. **Support Network:** Engage family, friends, and educators in supporting your child's interests.

Conclusion

Through their journey, the Sharma's learned that nurturing a child's potential is about providing opportunities, resources, and support while allowing space for exploration and growth. By balancing encouragement with flexibility, they helped Priya and Aarav discover and develop their talents, laying a foundation for lifelong learning and fulfilment.

Nurturing our Child's Potential

Identifying, developing, and encouraging a child's interests and talents is a dynamic process that can significantly impact their confidence, skills, and overall happiness. Here's how you can approach this:

Identifying Interests and Talents

1. **Observation:** Pay close attention to activities that naturally draw your child's attention. What do they enjoy doing in their free time? What subjects or activities do they seem passionate about or excel in?

- **Importance:** Early identification can help tailor their educational and extracurricular activities to match their interests, providing a more engaging and fulfilling experience.

- **Success Key:** Keep an open mind and avoid projecting your own interests onto your child. Their passions may be different from yours.

2. **Provide Exposure:** Introduce your child to a wide range of activities, subjects, and experiences. This could include sports, music, art, science kits, coding games, literature, and outdoor adventures.

- **Importance:** Exposure broadens their horizons and helps them discover passions they might not have encountered otherwise.

- **Success Key:** Offer these experiences without pressure or expectations. The goal is to let them explore freely.

3. **Listen and Communicate:** Engage in conversations about their likes and dislikes. Ask open-ended questions about what they enjoy and why.

- **Importance:** This shows that you value their opinions and encourages them to reflect on their interests.

- **Success Key:** Actively listen to their responses and validate their feelings, showing genuine interest in their thoughts.

Developing Interests and Talents

1. **Provide Resources:** Once you've identified a potential interest or talent, provide the tools and resources they need to explore and develop it further. This could include books, equipment, classes, or software.

- **Importance:** Access to the right resources can significantly accelerate learning and skill development.

- **Success Key:** Balance investment in resources with the child's sustained interest to avoid overwhelming them or placing undue financial burden on the family.

2. **Encourage Practice:** Support a routine that allows regular practice. Whether it's daily music practice, weekly art classes, or coding projects, consistency is key.

- **Importance:** Regular practice is crucial for skill development and mastery.

- **Success Key:** Help them set realistic goals and celebrate progress to maintain motivation.

3. **Seek Mentorship:** Connect your child with mentors or instructors who can provide guidance, inspiration, and advanced instruction in their area of interest.

- **Importance:** Mentors can offer expert advice, encouragement, and insights that parents may not be able to provide.

- **Success Key:** Choose mentors who are not only skilled but also good at communicating with and inspiring young people.

Encouraging Interests and Talents

1. **Celebrate Achievements:** Acknowledge both big accomplishments and small victories. This could be through verbal praise, a special family dinner, or showcasing their work.

- **Importance:** Recognition boosts self-esteem and reinforces the value of their efforts.

- **Success Key:** Make sure the celebration is proportional to the achievement to avoid creating undue pressure.

2. **Foster a Growth Mindset:** Teach them that skills and talents can be developed through hard work, perseverance, and learning from mistakes.

- **Importance:** A growth mindset encourages resilience and a positive attitude towards challenges.

- **Success Key:** Praise effort and progress rather than innate talent to encourage a focus on continuous improvement.

3. **Provide Opportunities for Application:** Look for opportunities where they can apply their skills and talents in real-world situations, such as community performances, competitions, or volunteering.

- **Importance:** Real-world applications provide valuable experience and can deepen their engagement with their interest.

- **Success Key:** Choose opportunities that are appropriate for their skill level to ensure a positive and encouraging experience.

General Considerations

- **Balance:** Ensure that focusing on interests and talents doesn't lead to an imbalanced lifestyle. Children should still have time for free play, relaxation, and socializing.

- **Adaptability:** Be prepared to shift focus if your child's interests change. It's normal for children to explore various passions as they grow.

- **Support Network:** Engage family, friends, and educators in supporting your child's interests. A supportive community can provide diverse opportunities and encouragement.

Here are some activity-based strategies to help achieve this, along with their importance and keys to success:

1. Observation and Exploration

- **Technique:** Pay close attention to what activities naturally draw your child's attention. Offer a variety of experiences, from art supplies and musical instruments to nature walks and sports equipment.

- **Importance:** This broad exposure helps identify your child's natural inclinations and interests.

- **Success Key:** Maintain an open and non-judgmental environment where the child feels free to explore different activities without the pressure of immediate success or proficiency.

2. Encouragement and Positive Reinforcement

- **Technique:** Provide positive feedback and encouragement when your child shows interest in an activity, regardless of their skill level. Focus on their effort and enjoyment rather than the outcome.

- **Importance:** Encouragement boosts confidence and motivation, making children more likely to continue developing their interests.

- **Success Key:** Genuine and specific praise (e.g., "I love the colors you used in your painting!") is more impactful than generic comments (e.g., "Good job!").

3. Structured and Unstructured Play

- **Technique:** Combine structured activities (classes, lessons) with unstructured play (free exploration). For example, enroll your child in a music class if they show interest in instruments but also allow them time to create their own music.

- **Importance:** Structured play provides skill development, while unstructured play fosters creativity and self-expression.

- **Success Key:** Balance is crucial. Too much structure can lead to burnout, while too little may not provide enough skill development.

4. Goal Setting and Small Achievements

- **Technique:** Help your child set achievable goals within their area of interest. Celebrate small milestones to encourage persistence.
- **Importance:** Goal setting teaches children the value of hard work and discipline in achieving success.
- **Success Key:** Ensure goals are attainable and age-appropriate to prevent frustration and maintain enthusiasm.

5. Role Models and Mentoring

- **Technique:** Introduce your child to role models who excel in their area of interest. This can be through books, videos, or ideally, personal interaction.
- **Importance:** Role models provide inspiration and a tangible example of what dedication to their interest can achieve.
- **Success Key:** Choose role models who not only excel in their field but also display qualities like perseverance, creativity, and humility.

6. Creative Challenges and Problem-Solving

- **Technique:** Present your child with challenges that require creative thinking and problem-solving within their interest area. For example, if they enjoy building, challenge them to create a structure that can support a certain weight.
- **Importance:** Challenges stimulate cognitive development and encourage innovative thinking.
- **Success Key:** Challenges should be stimulating but not so difficult that they lead to significant frustration.

7. Reflective Discussions

- **Technique:** Engage in discussions about what your child learned from their activities, what they found challenging, and what they enjoyed.

- **Importance:** Reflection helps children process their experiences, recognize their progress, and articulate their thoughts and feelings about their interests.
- **Success Key:** Encourage open-ended questions that prompt deeper thinking, rather than simple yes/no answers.

8. Collaborative Projects

- **Technique:** Encourage projects that involve collaboration with peers or family members, such as a group art project or a family science experiment.
- **Importance:** Collaborative projects teach teamwork, respect for others' ideas, and can enhance the enjoyment and depth of learning in their area of interest.
- **Success Key:** Ensure each participant has a role that contributes to the project's success, fostering a sense of belonging and accomplishment.

9. Flexibility and Adaptation

- **Technique:** Be prepared to adapt to your child's evolving interests. What starts as a passion for drawing might evolve into an interest in digital animation.
- **Importance:** Flexibility supports a child's natural curiosity and evolving identity.
- **Success Key:** Regularly check in with your child about their interests and be open to change, ensuring continuous engagement and growth.

10. Incorporation into Daily Life

- **Technique:** Integrate your child's interests into everyday life. For example, if they're interested in cooking, involve them in meal planning and preparation.
- **Importance:** This integration shows that their interests are valued and can be a meaningful part of their life.

- **Success Key:** The activity should be enjoyable and not feel like an obligation or chore, to maintain the child's enthusiasm.

By employing these techniques, you can effectively support your child's exploration and development of their interests and talents, laying a foundation for lifelong learning and personal fulfilment.

Nurturing Roots and Wings: Essance of Cultural Parenting

Story: Arjun's Journey: Nurturing Roots and Wings through Cultural Parenting

In a quaint village nestled in the lush hills of Uttarakhand, lived a young boy named Arjun. His family had deep roots in the region, and their traditions were intertwined with the rhythms of nature. Arjun's parents, Raj and Meera, believed in the importance of cultural and spiritual education, and they sought to raise him with a strong sense of identity and values.

Every morning, Raj and Meera took Arjun for a walk through the forest. As they walked, Raj would tell him stories from the Ramayana and Mahabharata, weaving in lessons about courage, kindness, and duty. These stories were more than just tales; they were a way to connect Arjun to his heritage and instil moral values.

One day, while walking through the forest, Raj pointed to a Banyan tree and said, "Arjun, this tree is sacred in our culture. It represents eternal life and wisdom. Just like this tree, our roots are strong, and they help us grow tall and wise."

Back home, Meera involved Arjun in gardening. They planted tulsi, marigold, and other plants significant in their rituals. She explained the importance of each plant, teaching him patience and responsibility. During festivals, they would use these flowers to decorate their home, making Arjun feel a deep connection to the traditions.

Every evening, the family practiced mindfulness and meditation. They sat in their courtyard, listening to the sounds of nature. Meera guided Arjun through simple breathing exercises and prayers. These sessions helped Arjun develop a sense of peace and self-awareness.

Arjun also learned about diverse cultures. His parents took him to local cultural events, where he experienced different music, dance, and food. They encouraged him to befriend children from different backgrounds, fostering an appreciation for diversity.

One day, Arjun's school organized a cultural exchange program. He was paired with a boy from a different state. They shared stories, traditions, and even tried cooking each other's favourite dishes. This experience broadened Arjun's perspective and deepened his empathy.

At home, discussions about cultural and spiritual matters were common. Raj and Meera encouraged Arjun to ask questions and express his thoughts. They believed that open dialogue was essential for his growth.

However, as Arjun grew older, he faced peer pressure. Some of his friends didn't understand or appreciate his cultural practices. They teased him for his traditional clothing and rituals. This made Arjun feel embarrassed and disconnected from his roots.

Sensing his turmoil, Raj and Meera decided to take Arjun on a special trip to Varanasi, the spiritual heart of their culture. They participated in the Ganga Aarti, visited ancient temples, and met people who lived by the values they cherished. This trip reignited Arjun's pride in his heritage.

On their return, Arjun shared his experiences with his friends, inviting them to join his family for a festival celebration. Seeing his enthusiasm and the beauty of the traditions, his friends' attitudes began to change. They became curious and more respectful of Arjun's cultural practices.

Years later, Arjun grew into a compassionate and confident young man, deeply rooted in his heritage and open to the world's diversity. He pursued a career in environmental conservation, inspired by his parents' teachings about respecting and protecting nature.

The Flip Side

Without such intentional cultural and spiritual education, Arjun might have struggled with his identity. He could have felt lost in a rapidly changing world, disconnected from his roots and values. The peer pressure might have led him to abandon his cultural practices altogether, creating a sense of emptiness and confusion about his place in the world.

Key Takeaways

1. **Cultural Heritage**: Sharing stories, language, and traditions creates a strong sense of identity and belonging.

2. **Spiritual Education:** Moral lessons, mindfulness, and meditation foster emotional and spiritual well-being.

3. **Diverse Exposure:** Experiencing different cultures broadens perspectives and fosters empathy.

4. **Open Dialogue:** Encouraging discussions about cultural and spiritual matters helps children develop critical thinking.

5. **Daily Integration:** Incorporating cultural and spiritual practices into daily life makes them a natural part of a child's experience.

6. **Community Engagement:** Participating in community and cultural events provides a sense of belonging and opportunities for learning.

By integrating cultural and spiritual education into parenting, we nurture well-rounded individuals who are rooted in their heritage, respectful of diversity, and equipped with the values and understanding to navigate the world.

Nurturing Roots and Wings: Essance of Cultural Parenting

Cultural and Spiritual Education plays a significant role in the parenting process, influencing not only the development of a child's identity and values but also their understanding and appreciation of their heritage and the diversity of the world around them. Including cultural and spiritual education in parenting can enhance a child's emotional intelligence, empathy, moral development, and sense of belonging. Here are some ways it can be integrated into the parenting process:

1. Sharing Cultural Heritage

- **Storytelling:** Parents can share stories, legends, and folklore from their cultural background, helping to pass on traditions, moral lessons, and cultural identity.

- **Language:** Teaching children the language of their cultural heritage can deepen their connection to their culture and broaden their communication skills.

- **Festivals and Traditions:** Participating in cultural festivals and practices as a family can create lasting memories and a deep sense of belonging.

2. Spiritual Education

- **Moral and Ethical Lessons:** Regardless of religious belief, parents can impart moral and ethical values through spiritual education, such as kindness, honesty, and respect for others.

- **Mindfulness and Meditation:** These practices can help children develop focus, peace, and self-awareness, contributing to their emotional and spiritual well-being.
- **Religious Teachings:** For those who follow a particular faith, sharing the teachings, stories, and values of that religion can provide a framework for understanding the world and making ethical decisions.

3. Exposure to Diverse Cultures

- **Cultural Events:** Attending cultural events, museums, and exhibitions can expose children to the rich tapestry of global cultures, fostering an appreciation for diversity.
- **Cultural Exchange:** Encouraging friendships with people from different backgrounds or participating in exchange programs can provide firsthand experience of other cultures.
- **Global Cuisine:** Introducing children to foods from various cultures can be a fun and engaging way to explore the world's diversity.

4. Discussion and Reflection

- **Open Dialogue:** Engaging in discussions about cultural and spiritual matters can encourage children to ask questions, express their thoughts, and develop critical thinking skills.
- **Reflective Practices:** Encouraging children to reflect on their experiences, beliefs, and the diversity around them can deepen their understanding and empathy.

5. Integration into Daily Life

- **Rituals and Daily Practices:** Incorporating cultural and spiritual rituals into daily life can make these elements a natural and constant part of a child's experience.
- **Art and Music:** Exposing children to the art and music of various cultures can enhance their artistic appreciation and understanding of different cultural expressions.

- **Books and Media:** Selecting books, films, and media that reflect diverse cultures and spiritual teachings can broaden a child's perspective and understanding.

6. Community Involvement

- **Community Service:** Participating in community service projects can teach children the value of compassion, empathy, and contributing to the greater good.
- **Religious or Cultural Institutions:** Engaging with local religious or cultural institutions can provide a sense of community and belonging, as well as opportunities for learning and service.

Incorporating cultural and spiritual education into parenting requires intentionality and openness. It's about creating an environment where children feel connected to their roots and respectful of others, equipped with the values and understanding to navigate a diverse world. This approach to parenting can help nurture well-rounded, empathetic, and culturally aware individuals.

Nature-based activities provide a unique and engaging way to integrate cultural and spiritual education into parenting. Here are some activities and tips for incorporating these lessons:

1. Nature Walks and Storytelling:

- **Activity:** Take regular walks in nature and use this time to tell stories from your cultural or spiritual heritage that relate to the natural world.
- **Importance:** This connects children with their roots and teaches them to respect and appreciate nature.
- **Tips:** Use local flora and fauna as characters in your stories or as symbols in cultural narratives.

2. Gardening and Learning About Native Plants:

- **Activity:** Involve children in gardening, focusing on plants that hold cultural or spiritual significance.

- **Importance:** It teaches responsibility, patience, and the cycle of life, while also connecting them to cultural traditions.
- **Tips:** Plant a garden with herbs, flowers, or plants used in your cultural or spiritual rituals and explain their significance.

3. **Observing and Participating in Seasonal Rituals:**
- **Activity:** Engage in seasonal rituals or celebrations that are significant to your culture or spiritual path, tied to natural cycles.
- **Importance:** It helps children understand the rhythm of nature and how it is reflected in human life and spirituality.
- **Tips:** Celebrate solstices, equinoxes, or traditional harvest festivals with activities that reflect your heritage.

4. **Mindfulness and Meditation in Nature:**
- **Activity:** Practice mindfulness or meditation with your children in a natural setting, perhaps using techniques or prayers from your spiritual tradition.
- **Importance:** This promotes mental well-being, connection to the present moment, and a sense of peace and interconnectedness with nature.
- **Tips:** Use simple, age-appropriate meditation or breathing techniques that children can easily follow.

5. **Art and Craft Using Natural Materials:**
- **Activity:** Collect natural materials during your outdoor activities to create art or crafts that reflect cultural symbols or stories.
- **Importance:** It fosters creativity and a hands-on connection with nature, while also delving into cultural heritage.
- **Tips:** Encourage the use of leaves, twigs, stones, and flowers to make traditional crafts or art pieces.

6. **Eco-friendly Practices as Spiritual Acts:**
- **Activity:** Teach children eco-friendly practices like recycling, composting, and conserving water as acts of respect for the Earth, which can be tied to spiritual beliefs about stewardship of the planet.
- **Importance:** It instils a sense of responsibility for the environment and can be linked to spiritual teachings about care for creation.
- **Tips:** Frame these practices within the context of your spiritual or cultural teachings about the Earth and our duty to protect it.

Incorporating cultural and spiritual education through nature-based activities not only enriches the parenting process but also fosters a deep connection between children, their heritage, and the environment. This holistic approach to parenting helps in nurturing well-rounded individuals who are aware of their cultural roots, spiritual beliefs, and the importance of nature in their lives.

Early Life Enrichment Gateway: A Foundations for a Fulfilling Life

"The Journey of Rohan: Foundations for a Fulfilling Life"

In the vibrant town of Madurai, nestled in the heart of Tamil Nadu, lived a young boy named Rohan. Rohan was a curious and spirited child, always eager to explore and learn. His family, though not wealthy, believed in the power of knowledge, hard work, and the simple joys of life.

Mood: To improve your mood, exercise

Rohan's father, a school teacher, encouraged him to start each day with a morning run through the fields surrounding their home. Initially, Rohan found it tiresome, but soon, the morning sun, the fresh air, and the rhythm of his heartbeat became a source of joy. Each day, as he returned from his run, he felt a surge of energy and happiness. The endorphins released during exercise lifted his spirits and set a positive tone for the rest of the day.

Clarity: To think more clearly, Meditate

Inspired by the teachings of ancient Indian sages, Rohan's grandmother introduced him to the practice of meditation. Every evening, they would sit together in a quiet corner of their home, focusing on their breath and chanting simple mantras. This practice helped Rohan calm his mind, reducing the noise and distractions that often clouded his thoughts. Over time, he found that meditation not only improved his concentration but also brought a sense of inner peace and clarity.

Knowledge: To understand the world, Read

Rohan's mother, a librarian, nurtured his love for reading. She brought home a variety of books – from local folklore to tales of distant lands. Rohan devoured them all, fascinated by the stories and the knowledge they imparted. Reading broadened his horizons, deepened his empathy, and ignited his imagination. He learned about different cultures, histories, and perspectives, which enriched his understanding of the world.

Self-Awareness: To understand yourself, Write

Inspired by the stories he read; Rohan began keeping a journal. Each night, he would jot down his thoughts, feelings, and experiences. This practice of writing helped him reflect on his day, understand his emotions, and set goals for the future. Through journaling, Rohan developed a deeper self-awareness and a clearer sense of his own identity and aspirations.

Self-Help: To help others, Help Yourself

Rohan's parents taught him the importance of self-care. They emphasized that to effectively help others, one must first take care of oneself. Rohan learned to prioritize his health, both physical and mental, by eating well, getting enough sleep, and taking time for activities he enjoyed. This self-care routine ensured he had the energy and emotional resilience to support and uplift those around him.

Learning: To learn faster, Have Fun

Rohan's best friend, Asha, shared his enthusiasm for learning. Together, they turned their studies into a game. They quizzed each other, created fun challenges, and related their lessons to real-life situations. This playful approach to learning made their studies enjoyable and helped them retain information better. They discovered that joy and curiosity were powerful catalysts for faster and more effective learning.

Growth: To grow faster, Stay Consistent

Rohan understood that consistency was key to personal growth. Inspired by his father's dedication to his work, Rohan developed a routine for his studies, hobbies, and self-improvement activities. He set clear goals and diligently worked towards them, tracking his progress and celebrating small victories. This consistency-built momentum and compounded his growth over time.

Love: To be loved, Love Others

One of the most profound lessons Rohan learned was the power of love and compassion. His family practiced kindness and empathy in their daily interactions, whether it was helping a neighbour in need or showing gratitude for small acts of kindness. Rohan embraced this principle wholeheartedly, performing random acts of kindness and actively listening to others. By expressing love and compassion, he built strong relationships and fostered a supportive community around him.

The Impact and Key Takeaways

Rohan's journey of integrating these foundational life-skills into his daily life transformed him into a well-rounded, empathetic, and knowledgeable individual. He experienced the joy of physical activity, the peace of meditation, the wisdom of reading, the self-awareness from writing, the importance of self-care, the fun in learning, the power of consistency, and the profound impact of love.

Key Takeaways:

1. **Start Small and Stay Consistent:** Incorporate these principles gradually and consistently into your daily routine.

2. **Find Joy in the Process:** Approach each activity with enthusiasm and make it enjoyable.

3. **Reflect and Adapt:** Regularly reflect on your progress and adapt your practices to suit your evolving needs.

4. **Foster Relationships:** Nurture meaningful relationships by showing love and compassion.

Early Life Enrichment Gateway:

A Foundations for a Fulfilling Life

"Foundations for a Fulfilling Life" represents a set of essential life-skills that, when followed, contribute to a happy and meaningful existence. These principles include:

1. **Mood:** Prioritizing physical activity through exercise to boost overall well-being.

2. **Clarity:** Cultivating mental clarity and peace through regular meditation practices.

3. **Knowledge:** Expanding one's understanding of the world and its complexities by reading and learning.

4. **Self-Awareness:** Enhancing self-knowledge and introspection through writing and reflection.

5. **Self-Help:** Recognizing the importance of self-care and personal growth as a means to help and support others effectively.

6. **Learning:** Approaching learning with enthusiasm and joy to accelerate personal development.

7. **Growth:** Achieving progress and personal development by maintaining consistency in one's efforts and actions.

8. **Love:** Nurturing meaningful relationships and fostering love and compassion for others.

These foundations collectively serve as a roadmap for individuals seeking to lead more fulfilling and purposeful lives by promoting holistic well-being, personal growth, and positive relationships.

Mean for Achieving the life-skills outlined in "Foundations for a Fulfilling Life" involves adopting a roadmap for personal development and well-being through adapting following basic activities and practice at early stage of our life.

Here's a roadmap to help you integrate these principles life lessons, explore activities that embody them, understand their impact, and consider key tips for incorporating them into daily life.

To improve your mood, exercise.

Activity: Engage in regular physical activities such as jogging, swimming, or even a brisk walk.

Impact: Exercise releases endorphins, known as 'feel-good' hormones, which can improve mood and decrease feelings of depression, anxiety, and stress.

Key Tips: Start with moderate activities you enjoy, aim for at least 30 minutes most days of the week, and make it a habit.

1. **To think more clearly, meditate.**
   - **Activity:** Practice mindfulness meditation, focusing on your breath or a mantra, to gain mental clarity.

- **Impact:** Meditation can reduce stress, enhance concentration, increase self-awareness, and promote emotional health.
- **Key Tips:** Begin with short sessions, even 5-10 minutes a day, in a quiet space where you won't be disturbed.

2. **To understand the world, read.**
- **Activity:** Read widely, including books, articles, and other materials from various cultures and perspectives.
- **Impact:** Reading broadens your understanding of the world, increases empathy, and improves cognitive functions.
- **Key Tips:** Set aside a reading time each day, keep a diverse reading list, and discuss what you read with others to deepen your understanding.

3. **To understand yourself, write.**
- **Activity:** Keep a journal and write regularly about your thoughts, feelings, and experiences.
- **Impact:** Writing can serve as a reflective practice that helps you understand your inner self, identify goals, and process emotions.
- **Key Tips:** Write consistently, be honest with your feelings, and use writing prompts if you're stuck.

4. **To help others, help yourself.**
- **Activity:** Engage in self-care practices to ensure you're at your best when assisting others.
- **Impact:** By taking care of your own needs, you can be more emotionally and physically available to support others.
- **Key Tips:** Prioritize your health, set boundaries to avoid burnout, and practice self-compassion.

5. **To learn faster, have fun.**
- **Activity:** Turn learning into a game or incorporate your interests into the process.

- **Impact:** Enjoyable learning experiences can improve memory and motivation, making the learning process more effective.
- **Key Tips:** Use educational games, relate new information to your hobbies, and don't be afraid to laugh at mistakes as part of the learning process.

6. **To grow faster, stay consistent.**
- **Activity:** Develop a routine or habit that contributes to personal growth, like a daily language lesson or skill practice.
- **Impact:** Consistency builds momentum, helps to form habits, and compounds growth over time.
- **Key Tips:** Set clear goals, track your progress, and establish a routine that aligns with your objectives.

7. **To be loved, love others.**
- **Activity:** Show kindness and compassion in your daily interactions with people.
- **Impact:** Expressing love and kindness to others can build strong relationships and foster a supportive community around you.
- **Key Tips:** Perform random acts of kindness, listen actively to others, and express gratitude regularly.

By integrating these activities and tips into your life, you can foster self-improvement and a deeper understanding of both yourself and the world around you.

The Silent Teachers: Understanding the Role of Role Models in Parenting

Story: "The Seeds of Tomorrow"

In a small village in India, there lived a family in which tradition was woven into everyday life. Ramesh and Priya, the parents, were known for their kindness and strong values. They had two children, Aarav and Meera, who looked up to their parents for guidance and inspiration.

Behavioral Modeling for Children

One morning, as the sun rose over the village, Ramesh took Aarav and Meera to the local market. The children watched as Ramesh patiently waited in line, smiling at everyone around him. When it was his turn, he greeted the vendor with respect and expressed gratitude for the fresh vegetables he bought. Aarav and Meera, observing their father's behaviour, started mimicking his polite manners and patience in their daily interactions, understanding the value of respect and patience.

Value and Belief Development

In the evenings, Priya often took the children to a nearby shelter where they volunteered to help the less fortunate. She explained the importance of community service and empathy. Aarav and Meera, inspired by their mother's dedication, began to understand the value of helping others and the joy it brought. They started initiating small acts of kindness in their school, like helping classmates and sharing their lunch with those who forgot theirs.

Inspiration and Motivation

Ramesh had always been passionate about science. One day, he showed Aarav and Meera his old science projects and spoke about his dreams of becoming an engineer, which he couldn't pursue due to financial constraints. His enthusiasm sparked a curiosity in Aarav, who started exploring science with a newfound interest, aspiring to achieve what his father couldn't. Priya, who loved gardening, shared her knowledge and passion with Meera, teaching her the importance of nurturing and patience, which Meera began applying to her studies and hobbies.

Socialization and Relationship Skills

Ramesh and Priya always made sure to listen to each other with empathy and understanding, even during disagreements. Aarav and Meera, observing their parents' respectful communication, learned to interact with their peers with the same level of empathy and understanding, fostering strong friendships and resolving conflicts peacefully.

Influence on Parenting Styles

Priya admired how her friend, Anjali, calmly handled her children's tantrums with patience and understanding. She started incorporating similar techniques at home, using calm and encouraging words when Aarav and Meera were upset, which led to a more peaceful and understanding family environment. Ramesh, noticing the positive changes, began adopting these techniques as well, enhancing their overall parenting style.

Problem-Solving Skills

One day, Aarav's toy broke, and he was heartbroken. Instead of buying a new one, Ramesh involved Aarav in fixing it. They brainstormed solutions together and managed to repair the toy. This experience taught Aarav valuable problem-solving skills and the importance of perseverance.

Career and Educational Aspirations

Priya celebrated her achievements at work with the family, sharing her excitement about her projects. This instilled a sense of value for education and hard work in Meera, who aspired to excel in her studies and pursue a career that she was passionate about.

Health and Well-being

Every morning, Ramesh led the family in a session of yoga and meditation, emphasizing the importance of physical activity and mental well-being. The family also took regular bike rides in the countryside, which became a cherished bonding activity and instilled in the children a positive attitude towards health and fitness.

Cultural and Social Identity

Priya and Ramesh made sure to celebrate festivals and cultural traditions with great enthusiasm, sharing stories of their heritage with Aarav and Meera. These celebrations helped the children understand and appreciate their cultural background, fostering a strong sense of identity and belonging.

Emotional and Psychological Support

Ramesh and Priya created a routine of bedtime stories, where they shared tales of courage, kindness, and wisdom. This routine provided emotional comfort and stability to Aarav and Meera, making them feel secure and loved.

The Flip Side: Lack of Positive Role Models

In a neighbouring household, things were different. Ravi, a local shopkeeper, often showed frustration and impatience in his interactions. His son, Rahul, observing his father's behaviour, started mimicking the same impatience and disrespect at school. Without positive role models, Rahul struggled with self-esteem and decision-making, often feeling lost and misunderstood.

Key Takeaways

1. **Behavioral Modeling:** Children learn behaviors through observation. Demonstrating patience, respect, and gratitude can significantly influence their conduct.

2. **Value Development:** Instilling values like empathy and community service can shape a child's character and world view.

3. **Inspiration and Motivation:** Sharing passions and struggles with children can inspire them to pursue their interests and develop resilience.

4. **Social Skills:** Role models teach children how to interact respectfully and empathetically, crucial for building strong relationships.

5. **Problem-Solving:** Involving children in problem-solving fosters critical thinking and independence.

6. **Health and Well-being:** Emphasizing physical activity and mental well-being instills lifelong healthy habits.

7. **Cultural Identity:** Celebrating cultural traditions helps children understand and appreciate their heritage.

8. **Emotional Support:** Consistent and positive role models provide emotional security and stability.

Conclusion

Role models play an indispensable role in parenting, shaping children's behaviours, values, and perspectives. By demonstrating positive behaviours and values, parents can profoundly influence their children's development, fostering well-rounded, resilient, and compassionate individuals. The presence of positive role models is crucial for effective parenting and child development

The Silent Teachers: Understanding the Role of Role Models in Parenting

Role models play a significant part in the parenting process, influencing both the parents' approaches to raising their children and the developmental outcomes of the children themselves. Role models play a crucial part in parenting, serving as a blueprint for behaviour, attitudes, and values for children. They can significantly influence a child's development, self-esteem, and decision-making skills. Here are some significations of role models in the process of parenting, along with illustrative examples for each:

1. **Behavioral Modeling for Children**

- **Imitation and Learning:** Children imitate behaviors they observe in their role models. For example, a child seeing their parent wait patiently in a queue may mimic this behavior at school, learning the value of patience and respect for turns.

- **Setting Standards:** Role models set behavioral and ethical standards. A parent who consistently expresses gratitude to service workers demonstrates to their child the importance of appreciation and respect for all forms of labor.

2. Value and Belief Development

- **Instilling Values:** Through observation, children adopt the values of their role models. Watching a role model volunteer at a local shelter can instill values of community service and empathy towards those in need in a child.

- **Influencing Beliefs:** Role models influence children's beliefs about themselves and the world. A role model discussing their failures and lessons learned can help a child develop a growth mindset, viewing setbacks as opportunities to learn.

3. Inspiration and Motivation

- **Aspirations:** Role models can inspire children to pursue their interests and goals. A child inspired by a parent or teacher passionate about science might aspire to explore a career in a related field.

- **Overcoming Challenges:** Observing role models work through difficulties teaches children resilience and problem-solving. For example, seeing a role model persistently address a household problem can teach a child the value of perseverance.

4. Socialization and Relationship Skills

- **Interpersonal Skills:** Children learn how to interact with others from their role models. A child observing their parent engaging in empathetic and active listening can learn the importance of these skills in building strong relationships.

- **Cultural and Social Norms:** Role models play a crucial role in teaching cultural values and social norms, helping children navigate their social environments. Participating in cultural traditions with role models can enhance a child's understanding and appreciation of their heritage.

5. Influence on Parenting Styles

- **Parental Learning:** Parents may adopt strategies from their role models, influencing their parenting styles. A parent admiring a friend's calm approach to handling tantrums might incorporate similar techniques into their discipline methods.

- **Adaptation and Growth:** Observing positive outcomes from role models can lead parents to adapt these strategies. For instance, a parent might use more encouragement and positive reinforcement after seeing their child's positive response to such methods from a teacher.

6. **Problem-Solving Skills**
- Role models show children how to approach and solve problems, fostering critical thinking and independence.
- **Example:** When a parent involves a child in fixing a broken toy by brainstorming solutions together, the child learns problem-solving skills and the value of perseverance.

7. **Career and Educational Aspirations**
- Children often look up to their parents' or other role models' achievements in education and career, which can inspire their own goals and aspirations.
- **Example:** A parent who shares their excitement about a work project or celebrates their educational achievements can inspire a child to value education and have aspirations for their own career.

8. **Interpersonal Relationships**
- The way role models interact with others provides a template for children's future relationships, teaching them about boundaries, respect, and communication.
- **Example:** When parents treat each other with respect and communicate effectively, even in disagreements, children learn the importance of respectful communication and emotional intelligence in relationships.

9. **Health and Well-being**
- Role models influence children's attitudes towards health, fitness, and overall well-being through their own habits and attitudes.

- Example: If a parent prioritizes physical activity by taking family bike rides or playing sports together, children are likely to adopt a positive attitude towards exercise and health.

10. Cultural and Social Identity

- Role models help children understand and connect with their cultural and social heritage, instilling a sense of pride and belonging.

- **Example:** Parents who celebrate cultural traditions and share stories of their heritage help children understand and appreciate their cultural background, fostering a strong sense of identity.

11. Emotional and Psychological Support

- **Security and Stability:** Consistent and positive role models provide a sense of security and stability. A routine like a bedtime story can offer emotional comfort and stability to a child.

- **Coping Mechanisms:** Children learn coping mechanisms by observing their role models. If a role model uses deep breathing or walking to calm down, a child can learn these as healthy ways to manage emotions.

Role models play a crucial role in parenting, especially when it comes to teaching children through activity-based techniques. Here are some significations of role models in parenting and tips for integrating these concepts into everyday activities:

1. Demonstrating Positive Behavior:

- **Significance:** Children learn by observing and mimicking the behavior of those around them. Parents and caregivers who model positive behaviors such as kindness, honesty, and perseverance set a practical example for children to follow.

- **Activity Tip:** Engage in community service or volunteer work together. This not only shows empathy and compassion in action but also provides a hands-on experience for children to learn the value of helping others.

2. Fostering Learning and Curiosity:

- **Significance:** When parents show excitement and curiosity about learning new things, it encourages a love of learning in children. This can lead to a lifelong pursuit of knowledge and personal growth.
- **Activity Tip:** Choose a new topic each week to explore together, such as space, ocean life, or different cultures. Use books, online resources, and hands-on projects to make learning fun and engaging.

3. Encouraging Resilience and Problem-Solving:

- **Significance:** Demonstrating how to face challenges and solve problems effectively teaches children resilience and critical thinking skills, preparing them for obstacles they may encounter in their own lives.
- **Activity Tip:** Work on puzzles, building projects, or challenging games together. Discuss the strategies you use to overcome obstacles and encourage your child to come up with their own solutions.

4. Promoting Physical Health and Activity:

- **Significance:** Parents who prioritize physical health, exercise, and proper nutrition serve as role models for maintaining a healthy lifestyle, which is crucial for physical and mental well-being.
- Activity Tip: Incorporate physical activities that can be done as a family, such as hiking, biking, or playing sports together. This not only promotes health but also provides quality family bonding time.

5. Instilling Social Skills and Empathy:

- **Significance:** Displaying good social skills and empathy in interactions with others teaches children how to communicate effectively and understand the feelings of others.
- **Activity Tip:** Participate in role-playing games where you and your child take turns portraying different emotions and situations. This can help develop empathy and improve communication skills.

6. Encouraging Creativity and Expression:

- **Significance:** When parents engage in creative activities and value artistic expression, it inspires children to explore their own creativity and find unique ways to express themselves.

- **Activity Tip:** Set aside time for arts and crafts, music, dance, or storytelling sessions where everyone can express themselves freely. Displaying your child's artwork or performing a mini-concert at home can boost their confidence.

7. Teaching Time Management and Responsibility:

- **Significance:** Modeling effective time management and responsibility shows children the importance of organization and accountability in achieving goals.

- **Activity Tip:** Involve your child in planning and scheduling family activities or chores. Use calendars or planning apps to teach them how to manage time and responsibilities.

By incorporating these activity-based techniques into your parenting, you can leverage the powerful influence of role models to teach valuable life skills and values, fostering the overall development of your child.

Conclusion

Role models, through their actions, behaviours, and values, have a profound impact on a child's development, shaping their behaviours, values, and perspectives on life. The presence of positive role models is indispensable in fostering well-rounded, resilient, and compassionate individuals, highlighting the critical role they play in effective parenting and child development.

Emotionally Intelligent Parenting: Boost our Child's Emotional IQ

Emotionally Intelligent Parenting: Boost our Child's Emotional IQ

Emotional Intelligence (EI) refers to the ability to recognize, understand, manage, and use one's own emotions positively to relieve stress, communicate effectively, empathize with others, overcome challenges, and defuse conflict. It also involves recognizing and understanding the emotions of others. EI plays a significant role in a child's overall development and is crucial in the parenting process. Here are key components of EI with examples and their importance:

Self-awareness

Illustrative Example: A child recognizes that they feel upset when they have to stop playing to do homework. They understand this emotion and can articulate it.

Importance: Self-awareness allows children to understand their feelings and the impact of their emotions on their behavior. This understanding is foundational for managing emotions and forming healthy relationships.

Self-regulation

Illustrative Example: Instead of throwing a tantrum when angry, a child learns to take deep breaths or count to ten to calm down.

Importance: Self-regulation helps children control their impulses and emotions, leading to more thoughtful decisions and actions. It's crucial for adapting to changing circumstances and dealing with frustrations.

Motivation

Illustrative Example: A child is motivated to complete their homework to have more time for play later, recognizing the value of delayed gratification.

Importance: Intrinsic motivation drives children to pursue goals and challenges without immediate rewards, fostering perseverance and a growth mindset.

Empathy

Illustrative Example: A child notices a classmate is sad about losing a game and offers kind words or suggests playing together to cheer them up.

Importance: Empathy enables children to understand and share the feelings of others, fostering compassion and building strong, supportive relationships.

Social Skills

Illustrative Example: A child learns to share toys and take turns, facilitating positive interactions and play with peers.

Importance: Good social skills enable children to communicate effectively, cooperate with others, navigate social complexities, and resolve conflicts constructively.

Importance in Child Development and Parenting

EI is crucial for a child's development as it underpins their ability to interact effectively with others, manage their own emotions, and navigate social situations. High EI is linked to better academic performance, healthier relationships, improved mental health, and greater career success.

In parenting, fostering EI involves modelling emotionally intelligent behaviour, providing opportunities for children to express their emotions, teaching them to identify and label their feelings, and guiding them through the process of managing emotions effectively. It also includes teaching empathy by encouraging children to consider others' perspectives and feelings.

By integrating EI into parenting practices, parents can help children develop a strong foundation of emotional understanding and regulation, setting the stage for lifelong well-being and success.

Emotional Intelligence: The Story of Aarav and His Family

Introduction

In a bustling city in India, lived Aarav, a curious and energetic 8-year-old boy. Aarav's parents, Priya and Rajesh, were both busy professionals who, despite their hectic schedules, were deeply committed to their son's well-being. They had recently attended a workshop on Emotional Intelligence (EI) and were inspired to incorporate EI practices into their parenting.

Story

A New Beginning

One sunny Sunday afternoon, Priya and Rajesh decided to introduce the concept of emotional intelligence to Aarav through a game of "Emotion Charades." They gathered in the living room, and Rajesh explained the rules: "We'll act out different emotions, and we all have to guess what they are."

Aarav was thrilled. He eagerly took his turn, acting out emotions like happiness, sadness, and anger with dramatic flair. Priya and Rajesh clapped and guessed each emotion, discussing each one afterward. They talked about situations that could cause these feelings and healthy ways to express them. Aarav learned that it was okay to feel angry but that throwing a tantrum wasn't the best way to handle it.

The Storytelling Twist

Later that week, during their nightly reading session, Priya read a story about a little boy named Ravi who had lost his favourite toy. She paused at key moments to ask Aarav how he thought Ravi felt and why. Aarav, engrossed in the story, shared his thoughts, empathizing with Ravi's sadness and frustration. Priya encouraged Aarav to think of alternative ways Ravi could have reacted, fostering empathy and self-reflection.

Artistic Expressions

One rainy day, Priya set up an art station in the living room. "Let's draw how we feel today," she suggested. Aarav excitedly grabbed his crayons and began to create a vibrant picture filled with swirling colours. Priya joined him, and they shared their artwork, discussing the emotions behind their creations. Aarav learned that art was a powerful way to express feelings without words.

The Emotion Wheel

Priya and Rajesh made an emotion wheel and hung it on the wall. Each evening, they took turns spinning the wheel and sharing stories about times they felt the selected emotion. Aarav learned to identify and articulate a wide range of feelings, from joy to jealousy. This activity helped him understand that all emotions are valid and that talking about them is essential.

Role-Playing Scenarios

On weekends, the family engaged in role-playing games. They acted out scenarios like resolving a conflict with a friend or dealing with disappointment. After each role-play, they discussed different strategies and their outcomes. Aarav learned to navigate social situations with empathy and emotional regulation.

Mindfulness Moments

Every morning, the family practiced mindfulness together. They sat quietly, focusing on their breath and being aware of their emotions and sensations. This practice helped Aarav stay calm and centred, even during stressful moments.

Gratitude Journaling

Each night, before bed, Aarav wrote in his gratitude journal. He jotted down things he was thankful for, from a fun day at school to a delicious meal. Priya and Rajesh shared their gratitude lists too, modelling positive behaviour and fostering a sense of appreciation.

The Flip Side

While Priya and Rajesh's efforts bore fruit, they also faced challenges. Sometimes, Aarav resisted discussing his feelings, especially when he was upset. There were moments when their busy schedules made it difficult to maintain consistency in their EI practices. Priya and Rajesh realized that developing emotional intelligence was an ongoing process that required patience and perseverance.

Key Takeaways

1. **Self-Awareness:** Encourage children to recognize and articulate their emotions. This helps them understand the impact of their feelings on their behaviour.

2. **Self-Regulation:** Teach children techniques like deep breathing or counting to ten to manage their emotions. This fosters impulse control and thoughtful decision-making.

3. **Motivation:** Help children set goals and understand the value of delayed gratification. This builds intrinsic motivation and perseverance.

4. **Empathy:** Encourage children to consider others' perspectives and feelings. This develops compassion and strong, supportive relationships.

5. **Social Skills:** Provide opportunities for children to practice sharing, taking turns, and resolving conflicts. This enhances their ability to navigate social situations effectively.

Conclusion

Priya and Rajesh's journey to boost Aarav's emotional intelligence was filled with learning and growth. By incorporating EI practices into their daily lives, they created a nurturing environment where Aarav could thrive emotionally. They learned that while challenges were inevitable, the benefits of fostering emotional intelligence far outweighed the difficulties. Aarav grew into a compassionate, resilient, and emotionally intelligent individual, ready to face the world with confidence and empathy.

Emotional Intelligence (EI) Parenting Process Through Activities and Games

Incorporating Emotional Intelligence (EI) into the parenting process through activities and games can be both effective and enjoyable. These techniques can help children learn to understand and manage their emotions, empathize with others, and develop social skills. Here are some activity-based techniques, along with keys to success and tips:

1. Emotion Charades

- **Activity:** Play a game of charades where instead of movies or books, the themes are emotions. Children can act out different emotions, and others guess what they are.
- **Key to Success:** Encourage children to think about how different emotions can be expressed through facial expressions, body language, and actions.
- **Tip:** Discuss the emotions afterward—talk about what can cause these feelings and healthy ways to express them.

2. Storytelling with Emotional Twists

- **Activity:** Tell a story or read a book together, and then discuss the emotions of different characters at various points in the story. You can also create alternative endings based on different emotional responses.

- **Key to Success:** Use open-ended questions to explore why characters might feel a certain way and how different actions reflect their emotions.

- **Tip:** Encourage children to relate the characters' experiences to their own, fostering empathy and self-reflection.

3. Emotional Artwork

- **Activity:** Provide art supplies and ask children to create artwork based on different emotions they've experienced. They can use colors, shapes, and images to express how they felt.

- **Key to Success:** Discuss the artwork without judgment, focusing on understanding the emotions and thoughts behind the creations.

- **Tip:** Use this as an opportunity to discuss that all emotions are valid and there are healthy ways to express and manage them.

4. The Emotion Wheel

- **Activity:** Create an emotion wheel with various emotions displayed around a circle. Have children spin the wheel and then talk about or act out a time they felt that emotion.

- **Key to Success:** Validate all emotional expressions and use this as a learning moment to discuss appropriate emotional responses and empathy.

- **Tip:** Use diverse and complex emotions to expand emotional vocabulary and understanding.

5. Role-Playing Scenarios

- **Activity:** Create role-playing scenarios that involve navigating social situations, such as resolving a conflict, dealing with a disappointment, or helping a friend in need.
- **Key to Success:** Debrief after each role-play to discuss different strategies and their outcomes, focusing on emotional regulation and empathy.
- **Tip:** Encourage children to consider multiple perspectives and possible solutions to enhance problem-solving and empathy.

6. Mindfulness and Emotion Regulation Activities

- **Activity:** Practice mindfulness techniques like deep breathing, meditation, or yoga together, focusing on being aware of one's emotions and body sensations.
- **Key to Success:** Make mindfulness a regular practice and relate it back to emotional regulation during stressful or emotional moments.
- **Tip:** Use simple and engaging mindfulness activities suited to the child's age to keep them interested and involved.

7. Gratitude Journaling

- **Activity:** Encourage children to keep a gratitude journal where they can write or draw things, they are thankful for each day.
- **Key to Success:** Share your own gratitude lists to model positive behavior and discuss the emotional impact of focusing on positive aspects of life.
- **Tip:** Make it a daily or weekly routine, which can help in developing a positive outlook and emotional resilience.

Keys to Success & Tips

1. **Be a Role Model:** Demonstrate emotional intelligence in your own behavior. Children learn a lot by observing adults.

2. **Open Communication:** Foster an environment where emotions can be openly discussed without judgment.

3. **Emotional Vocabulary:** Regularly use and teach a wide range of emotion words to help children articulate their feelings accurately.

4. **Empathize:** Show empathy towards your child's emotions, validating their feelings and showing understanding.

5. **Consistency:** Incorporate these activities regularly to reinforce learning and make EI a natural part of daily life.

Incorporating these activities into your parenting can make learning about emotions fun and engaging for children, laying a strong foundation for emotional intelligence that will benefit them throughout their lives.

Emotionally Safe Parenting: Valuing, Understanding, And Securing Children's Growth

Emotionally Safe Parenting: Valuing, Understanding, and Securing Children's Growth

Emotionally safe parenting refers to a parenting style that creates a secure, supportive, and nurturing environment for children, enabling them to express their feelings and thoughts without fear of judgment, rejection, or punishment. This approach focuses on understanding and responding to children's emotional needs, fostering their emotional intelligence, and helping them develop healthy coping mechanisms for stress and challenges. Emotionally safe parenting is grounded in empathy, open communication, respect, and unconditional love. Key factors of emotionally safe parenting include:

1. **Empathy and Understanding:** Recognizing and validating children's emotions, showing that you understand their feelings, and conveying that their emotions are important.
- **Example:** When a child is upset about losing a game, an emotionally safe parent might say, "It sounds like you're really disappointed about the game. It's okay to feel upset when things don't go the way we hoped."

2. **Open Communication:** Encouraging children to express their thoughts and feelings openly, without fear of negative consequences, and actively listening to what they say.
- **Example:** A parent notices their child seems quiet after school and asks, "You seem a bit quiet today, is there anything on your mind you'd like to talk about?"

3. **Consistent Support and Nurturance:** Providing consistent emotional and physical support, making children feel secure and loved unconditionally, regardless of their actions or achievements.
- **Example:** Celebrating the effort a child puts into a project, regardless of the outcome, and reassuring them of your love and support even when they make mistakes.

4. **Setting Healthy Boundaries:** Establishing clear, reasonable rules and expectations that are communicated respectfully and enforced consistently, helping children understand limits and develop self-discipline.
- **Example:** A parent might explain to a child why bedtime is set at a certain time, emphasizing the importance of rest for health and well-

being, and consistently enforcing this rule in a gentle but firm manner.

5. **Modelling Emotional Regulation:** Demonstrating how to manage and express emotions in a healthy way, showing children through your own behaviour how to cope with stress, frustration, and disappointment.
   - **Example:** When a parent is frustrated by a work email, they might say, "I'm feeling pretty frustrated by this message. I'm going to take a few deep breaths and think about it before I respond."

6. **Encouraging Independence while Providing Guidance:** Allowing children to make choices and solve problems on their own when appropriate, while being available to offer guidance and support when needed.
   - **Example:** Letting a child choose their own outfit for the day but offering help if they ask for it, or letting them work on homework independently while making it clear you're there to help if needed.

7. **Respecting Individuality:** Recognizing and celebrating each child's unique personality, interests, and strengths, and avoiding comparisons with siblings or peers.
   - **Example:** If one child excels in sports and another in art, the parent applauds each child's achievements and interests without drawing comparisons, acknowledging each child's individual talents and passions.

Emotionally safe parenting is about balancing warmth and structure, providing a secure base from which children can explore the world, learn from their experiences, and develop into emotionally healthy adults. It requires self-awareness and self-regulation on the part of the parent, as well as a commitment to ongoing learning and growth in the parent-child relationship.

Story: Beneath the Banyan: Nurturing Emotionally Safe Parenting

In a quaint village in India, nestled between lush green fields and flowing rivers, lived a family that epitomized warmth and togetherness. The family consisted of Arjun, a gentle father who worked as a teacher, Meera, a nurturing mother who loved to cook and garden, and their two children, Riya, a curious and imaginative girl of 10, and Karan, an energetic and adventurous boy of 7.

Arjun and Meera believed in the power of emotionally safe parenting, creating a secure and supportive environment for their children. They often spent weekends exploring the nearby forest, where an ancient banyan tree stood as a symbol of strength and wisdom. The tree, with its sprawling roots and expansive canopy, became a magical place for the family to bond, learn, and grow together.

One sunny morning, Arjun and Meera decided to take Riya and Karan on a nature walk to the banyan tree. As they walked, Arjun noticed that Karan seemed unusually quiet. He gently asked, "Karan, you seem a bit quiet today. Is there something on your mind you'd like to talk about?" Karan hesitated for a moment but then opened up about a game he had lost at school. "I felt so bad, Papa. Everyone was cheering for the other team."

Arjun knelt down to Karan's level, placing a comforting hand on his shoulder. "It sounds like you're really disappointed about the game. It's okay to feel upset when things don't go the way we hoped. Remember, it's not just about winning, but about trying your best and learning from each experience."

As they reached the banyan tree, Meera suggested a "trust walk." She blindfolded Riya and asked Karan to guide her around the tree, emphasizing the importance of trust and clear communication. Riya giggled nervously at first but soon felt secure with Karan's guidance. "I trust you, Karan," she said, and Karan beamed with pride.

Later, they sat under the tree, creating nature journals. Meera encouraged the children to draw or write about their feelings and experiences in nature. Riya drew a picture of the banyan tree, symbolizing strength and security, while Karan wrote about the trust walk and how it made him feel responsible and trusted.

To foster mindfulness, Arjun led a listening session, asking everyone to close their eyes and focus on the sounds around them – the rustling leaves, chirping birds, and distant river flow. "What do you hear?" he asked. "Birds singing," Riya whispered. "Leaves dancing," Karan added. The exercise helped them feel connected to nature and relaxed.

As the day went on, they built a small shelter using fallen branches and leaves, encouraging the children to solve problems and be resourceful. "This is fun!" Karan exclaimed. "Look how strong our shelter is!" Arjun and Meera praised their efforts, reinforcing the value of resilience and adaptability.

Before heading home, they observed animals through binoculars, discussing how animals might feel in different situations. "Imagine how the deer feels when it sees us," Meera suggested. "Scared or curious?" This activity nurtured empathy in the children, teaching them to understand and connect with other living beings.

Back home, the lessons from their day continued. During bedtime, Arjun explained why a regular sleep schedule was important, setting healthy boundaries with a gentle but firm tone. Meera celebrated the effort Riya put into her art project, regardless of the outcome, reassuring her of their unconditional love and support.

Flip Side:

In a parallel story, a neighbouring family struggled with a different approach. The parents, busy with work and stressed about daily life, often dismissed their children's feelings. When little Anika lost a game, her father's response was, "It's just a game. Stop crying." This lack of empathy made Anika feel invalidated and insecure.

The parents rarely engaged in open communication. When Anika seemed quiet, no one asked why. She bottled up her emotions, feeling misunderstood and alone. The lack of consistent support and nurturance left her yearning for validation and love.

Without healthy boundaries, Anika stayed up late watching TV, affecting her sleep and health. When her parents set rules, they were inconsistent and enforced harshly, causing confusion and resentment.

Anika missed out on learning emotional regulation, as her parents often displayed anger and frustration without managing their emotions. She struggled with her feelings, unable to develop healthy coping mechanisms.

Unlike Riya and Karan, Anika's independence was stifled. Her parents made decisions for her, not allowing her to choose her own path. Her individuality was overlooked, as comparisons with her siblings eroded her self-esteem.

Key Takeaways:

1. **Empathy and Understanding:** Validate children's emotions and show understanding to make them feel valued and secure.

2. **Open Communication:** Encourage children to express their thoughts and feelings openly, fostering trust and connection.

3. **Consistent Support and Nurturance:** Provide unwavering emotional and physical support, reinforcing unconditional love.

4. **Setting Healthy Boundaries:** Establish clear, reasonable rules and expectations, helping children understand limits and develop self-discipline.

5. **Modelling Emotional Regulation:** Demonstrate healthy emotional management, teaching children to cope with stress and frustration.

6. **Encouraging Independence:** Allow children to make choices and solve problems, fostering confidence and self-reliance.

7. **Respecting Individuality:** Celebrate each child's unique personality and strengths, avoiding comparisons.

By incorporating emotionally safe parenting and nature-based activities, parents can create a nurturing environment where children thrive emotionally, mentally, and physically. The banyan tree of love symbolizes the strength and wisdom needed to foster such an environment, guiding children to become emotionally healthy and resilient adults.

Top of Form

Emotionally safe parenting is crucial for the healthy emotional development of children. It involves creating an environment where children feel valued, understood, and secure. Integrating nature-based activities and games can enhance this emotional safety by connecting children to the natural world, promoting relaxation, and encouraging exploration and learning in a calming environment. Below are ten significances of emotionally safe parenting through nature-based activities, along with suggested activities, their importance, and tips for each:

1. **Building Trust and Security:**
- **Activity:** Nature walks with a "trust walk" component, where one child is blindfolded and guided by another.
- **Importance:** Helps children develop trust in others and feel secure in their environment.

- **Tips:** Always ensure safety during the trust walk and encourage gentle guidance and clear communication.

2. **Enhancing Emotional Awareness:**
- **Activity:** Creating nature journals where children can draw or write about their feelings and experiences in nature.
- **Importance:** Encourages children to express and understand their emotions.
- **Tips:** Provide a variety of materials and suggest they use colours and symbols to express different emotions.

3. **Promoting Mindfulness and Relaxation:**
- **Activity:** Mindful listening sessions in nature, focusing on different sounds like bird calls or rustling leaves.
- **Importance:** Helps children practice mindfulness and find relaxation in the natural world.
- **Tips:** Encourage children to close their eyes and breathe deeply, focusing solely on the sounds around them.

4. **Fostering Resilience and Adaptability:**
- **Activity:** Building shelters or forts with natural materials.
- **Importance:** Teaches children to adapt to challenges and be resourceful.
- **Tips:** Encourage creativity and problem-solving, allowing children to lead the project with minimal adult intervention.

5. **Encouraging Empathy and Connectedness:**
- **Activity:** Animal watching and discussing how animals might feel in different situations.
- **Importance:** Develops empathy by understanding and connecting with other living beings.
- **Tips:** Use binoculars for observing wildlife from a distance and discuss animals' behaviours and possible emotions.

6. **Stimulating Curiosity and Exploration:**
- **Activity:** Nature scavenger hunts with items to find or observe.
- **Importance:** Encourages a sense of wonder and exploration.
- **Tips:** Create a diverse list that includes both easy and challenging items to find, catering to different age groups.

7. **Developing Social Skills:**
- **Activity:** Group gardening projects, where children work together to plant and care for a garden.
- **Importance:** Teaches cooperation, communication, and responsibility.
- **Tips:** Assign specific tasks to each child and rotate roles to ensure everyone learns and participates in different aspects of gardening.

8. **Enhancing Physical Health:**
- **Activity:** Nature-based obstacle courses or tree climbing under supervision.
- **Importance:** Promotes physical activity and health in a fun, engaging way.
- **Tips:** Ensure safety measures are in place and adapt activities to suit children's age and physical abilities.

9. **Supporting Cognitive Development:**
- **Activity:** Nature-based treasure hunts with clues related to natural elements (e.g., find a rock that looks like it has layers).
- **Importance:** Enhances problem-solving skills and cognitive development.
- **Tips:** Make clues age-appropriate and encourage teamwork to solve them.

10. Promoting Environmental Stewardship:

- **Activity:** Participating in local clean-up days or starting a recycling project.
- **Importance:** Instils a sense of responsibility and care for the environment.
- **Tips:** Discuss the impact of their actions on the environment and encourage them to come up with ideas for sustainable practices.

Incorporating these nature-based activities into parenting not only fosters emotional safety but also connects children with the natural world, promoting overall well-being and development. Remember to always prioritize safety, provide encouragement, and allow children to explore at their own pace for a truly enriching experience.

Individuality vs. Obedience: Balancing Act for Crafting Well-Rounded Children in Today's Competitive Environment

Story: The Banyan Tree and the Kite: A Tale of Individuality and Obedience

Story:

In the heart of a bustling Indian village stood a grand old banyan tree. Its thick roots anchored it firmly to the ground, and its vast branches provided shelter to countless birds and animals. The banyan tree was known for its wisdom, accumulated over centuries of observing the world. Nearby, a young boy named Aarav loved to visit the tree, bringing with him his colourful kite, which he had crafted with his own hands.

Aarav was known for his unique ideas and fearless spirit. He often came up with unconventional projects and loved experimenting, much like the time he built a small windmill out of recycled materials. However, his strong individuality sometimes clashed with the expectations of his school and his strict father, who valued discipline and obedience.

One day, Aarav's father asked him to participate in a science fair. While his classmates chose well-trodden paths for their projects, Aarav decided to design a kite that could generate electricity. His father, worried about Aarav's tendency to deviate from the norm, insisted he pick a simpler, more conventional project. Aarav reluctantly agreed but couldn't abandon his dream.

That afternoon, as Aarav sat under the banyan tree, the old tree whispered to him, "Aarav, sometimes roots and wings need to work together. The kite must rise high, but it must also be tethered to the ground."

Inspired, Aarav decided to work on both projects. He completed the conventional project his father approved, ensuring he followed all the guidelines and rules. Simultaneously, he worked on his kite in secret, pouring his creativity and individuality into it.

The day of the science fair arrived. Aarav presented his approved project, which received decent praise. However, he couldn't resist unveiling his kite. As he launched it into the sky, the kite not only soared high but also lit up a small bulb connected to it, demonstrating his innovative idea of generating electricity. The crowd was astonished, and his father, initially apprehensive, felt a surge of pride.

Aarav's teacher, impressed by his dual approach, gathered the children and told them the story of the banyan tree and the kite. "Aarav has shown us the importance of balancing individuality and obedience. He followed the rules and completed the assigned project, demonstrating obedience. But he also pursued his unique idea, showing individuality. Both traits are essential for success."

Key Takeaways:

1. **Balance:** Encourage children to balance individuality and obedience. Aarav's story illustrates that adhering to necessary norms doesn't hinder creativity but can coexist with it.

2. **Encourage Exploration:** Allow children to explore their interests and ideas, even if they diverge from the norm. Aarav's kite project was unconventional but innovative.

3. **Teach Critical Thinking:** Children should be encouraged to question and think critically about the 'why' behind rules and norms. Aarav didn't just follow instructions blindly; he understood the importance of both his projects.

4. **Model Respectful Disagreement:** Teach children how to express their opinions and disagreements respectfully. Aarav's respectful approach to his father's wishes while still pursuing his idea demonstrates this.

5. **Supportive Environment:** Create an environment that values both individual expression and understanding of rules. Aarav's success was partly due to the wisdom and support he found under the banyan tree.

6. **Open Communication:** Maintain open lines of communication, encouraging children to express themselves. Aarav's discussions with the banyan tree symbolize the importance of finding a safe space to express one's thoughts.

Individuality vs. Obedience: Balancing Act for Crafting Well-Rounded Children in Today's Competitive Environment:

The differences between children with strong individuality and obedient children can be significant, especially in today's challenging and competitive times. Each trait has its importance, potential drawbacks, and ways in which it can be nurtured. Here's a detailed explanation, along with illustrative examples, tips for success, and suggested parenting approaches:

Differences

1. **Expression vs. Compliance**
- **Individuality:** Children with strong individuality often express their thoughts, feelings, and preferences clearly and assertively. They're likely to question norms and think critically.
- **Obedience:** Obedient children tend to follow rules and guidelines without much questioning. They value compliance and are often eager to please adults and authority figures.

2. **Risk-Taking vs. Risk-Aversion**
- **Individuality:** These children may be more willing to take risks and try new things, viewing failures as learning opportunities.
- **Obedience:** Obedient children might avoid risks to adhere to rules or avoid disapproval, potentially missing out on growth opportunities.

3. **Innovation vs. Conformity**
- **Individuality:** Children with strong individuality can be more innovative and creative, thinking outside the box.
- **Obedience:** Obedient children might prefer sticking to established methods and norms, which can limit creative development.

Importance
- Individuality is crucial for fostering creativity, leadership, and adaptability. Children with strong individuality can navigate

complex social and academic environments effectively, finding unique solutions to problems.

- Obedience is important for ensuring safety, understanding the value of structure, and developing the ability to work within teams and follow necessary instructions.

Drawbacks

- **Individuality:** Without guidance, strong individuality can sometimes lead to clashes with authority, difficulty in group settings where conformity is needed, or an unwillingness to compromise.
- **Obedience:** Excessive obedience might stifle self-expression and critical thinking, potentially leading to a lack of initiative or dependency on external validation.

Illustrative Examples

- An individually strong child might decide to work on an unconventional project for a science fair, exploring new ideas and methodologies, which demonstrates innovation but might also risk failure or criticism.
- An obedient child might choose a well-trodden project path, ensuring approval and possibly success within established parameters but missing out on personal interest exploration and creative growth.

Tips and Keys to Success

1. **Balance:** Encourage a balance between individuality and obedience to foster a well-rounded personality capable of critical thinking yet respectful of necessary norms.

2. **Encourage Exploration:** Allow children to explore their interests and ideas, even if they diverge from the norm, to support individuality.

3. **Teach Critical Thinking:** Encourage children to ask questions and think critically about the 'why' behind rules and norms.

4. **Model Respectful Disagreement:** Teach children how to express their opinions and disagreements respectfully, showing that individuality doesn't mean disregard for others' views.

Suggested Parenting Approach

1. **Supportive Environment**: Create an environment that values both individual expression and the understanding of rules. Recognize and celebrate unique traits while explaining the importance of certain rules and cooperation.

2. **Open Communication:** Maintain open lines of communication, encouraging children to express themselves and discuss their thoughts on obedience and rules.

3. **Guidance and Autonomy:** Provide guidance when necessary but also allow for autonomous decision-making within safe boundaries to foster responsible individuality.

4. **Encourage Empathy:** Teach the importance of understanding and considering others' feelings and perspectives, blending individuality with social harmony.

Balancing strong individuality with the ability to be obedient, when necessary, can prepare children to navigate the complexities of modern life effectively, making them adaptable, respectful, and innovative individuals.

Activity-Based Strategies for Balancing Individuality and Obedience

To foster a balance between individuality and obedience in children, activity-based games and techniques can be both effective and engaging. Here are some suggestions, along with their importance and tips for implementation:

1. Role-Playing Games

Activity: Create scenarios where children play different roles, some requiring them to follow specific instructions (obedience) and others allowing them to make their own rules or solve problems creatively (individuality).

Importance: Role-playing helps children understand the value of different perspectives and contexts, teaching them when it's important to follow rules and when they can express their individuality.

Tips:

- Encourage reflection after each role-play to discuss what they learned about following rules and being creative.
- Swap roles frequently to ensure children experience both sides of the spectrum.

2. Group Projects with Assigned Roles

Activity: Organize group projects where each child is assigned a role that requires them to adhere to certain guidelines (obedience), but also offers the freedom to contribute ideas and solutions within their role (individuality).

Importance: This activity teaches the balance between contributing personal strengths to a group while respecting the structure and roles within the team.

Tips:

- Rotate roles in different projects to give each child a chance to lead and follow.
- Set clear objectives but allow the children to decide how to achieve them, encouraging innovation within boundaries.

3. Creative Arts Workshops

Activity: Conduct workshops focusing on art, music, or writing, where children are given a theme (boundary) but can express it in any form they choose (individuality).

Importance: Creative arts encourage self-expression and individuality within a given framework, balancing freedom and structure.

Tips:

- Offer a variety of materials and mediums to explore.
- Discuss the theme and guidelines clearly, then let the children's creativity take the lead.

4. Structured Debate Clubs

Activity: Set up a debate club where children learn to research and defend a position (individuality) while also following debate rules and respecting opposing viewpoints (obedience).

Importance: Debating fosters critical thinking and the ability to articulate personal views while adhering to a structured format and listening to others.

Tips:

- Choose topics that are age-appropriate and engaging.
- Teach respectful listening and response techniques to ensure a constructive environment.

5. Problem-Solving Challenges

Activity: Design challenges or puzzles that children must solve within certain constraints or using specific tools (obedience), but encourage creative solutions (individuality).

Importance: Problem-solving within constraints teaches children to think creatively while respecting necessary boundaries.

Tips:

- Use real-world problems to increase engagement and relevance.
- Encourage teamwork and share different approaches to the same problem.

6. Nature Exploration Activities

Activity: Engage children in outdoor activities that involve exploring nature, such as scavenger hunts, identifying plant and animal species, or building natural shelters.

Importance: These activities foster a sense of wonder and curiosity about the world, crucial for individuality. They also teach respect for nature's rules and the importance of following safety guidelines, illustrating obedience's value in certain contexts.

Tips:

- Allow children the freedom to explore and ask questions, guiding them to find answers independently or in small groups.
- Discuss the importance of respecting nature and following environmental guidelines during these activities, reinforcing the concept of responsible obedience.

7. Interactive Storytelling Sessions

Activity: Host storytelling sessions where children can contribute to a collective story, each adding their twist (individuality) but must follow the plotline or theme established by the previous storyteller (obedience).

Importance: This activity encourages creative expression within the continuity and rules of the collective story.

Tips:

- Start with a compelling story setup to spark interest.
- Guide the session to ensure the story remains coherent while allowing for diverse contributions.

Implementation Tips:

- **Foster a Safe Environment:** Ensure that all activities are conducted in a supportive atmosphere where children feel safe to express themselves and explore.
- **Provide Constructive Feedback:** Offer positive reinforcement and constructive feedback to encourage learning and growth.
- **Encourage Reflection:** After each activity, engage children in a discussion about what they learned and how they felt about the balance between following rules and expressing themselves.

- **Adapt to Individual Needs:** Be mindful of each child's comfort level and adapt activities to ensure they are inclusive and engaging for everyone.

By integrating these activities into educational or recreational programs, children can develop a healthy balance between individuality and obedience, critical for their personal and social development.

Life's Journey: A Guide to Effective Parenting and Healthy Relationships

Building Bridges: Crossing Parent-Child Conflicts with Creative Solutions

Story: "Navigating the Tides of Change: An Inspirational Journey of a Parent-Child Relationship in India"

Introduction

In a bustling Indian city, lived the Sharma family. Rajesh Sharma, a diligent father, and Meera Sharma, a compassionate mother, were raising their two children, Aarav and Ananya. As Aarav transitioned into adolescence and Ananya into her teenage years, the Sharma family found themselves navigating a sea of conflicts, typical yet challenging. This is their story of understanding, overcoming, and growing through these conflicts with love and creativity.

Developmental Changes

Conflict: Aarav, now 13, began seeking more independence, leading to clashes with Rajesh over curfews and social outings. Activity: Goal-setting Workshop Story: One evening, after another heated argument about curfews, Rajesh and Aarav sat down with a large sheet of paper and colourful markers. They created a vision board together, outlining Aarav's aspirations and the responsibilities that came with increased freedom. As they set realistic milestones, Rajesh realized the importance of gradually letting go, while Aarav understood the value of earning trust.

Key Tips: Ensure goals are realistic and achievable to maintain motivation. Celebrate each achieved milestone to reinforce positive development.

Differing Expectations

Conflict: Meera expected Ananya to excel in academics and participate in household chores, but Ananya felt overwhelmed by the pressure. **Activity:** Family Contract **Story:** Meera, Rajesh, and Ananya sat around the dining table to draft a "family contract." They each voiced their expectations and responsibilities, ensuring everyone's opinions were heard. By the end of the evening, they had a clear, written agreement that balanced academic expectations with Ananya's need for relaxation and personal time.

Key Tips: Review and revise the contract periodically to reflect changes in circumstances or expectations. Use positive language to frame responsibilities and consequences.

Communication Styles

Conflict: Rajesh preferred a directive communication style, while Aarav sought a more collaborative approach. **Activity:** Role-reversal Exercise Story: During a family meeting, they decided to switch roles. Aarav acted as the parent, and Rajesh as the child. This exercise was eye-opening for both, fostering empathy and understanding. Rajesh learned to listen more, and Aarav appreciated the challenges of parenting.

Key Tips: Encourage honest expression during role-play without judgment. Discuss the insights gained from the experience to enhance understanding.

Discipline and Behavior Management

Conflict: Ananya felt that her parents' disciplinary actions were inconsistent and unfair. **Activity:** Problem-solving Board Game **Story:** Together, the Sharma's designed a board game that reflected real-life challenges and consequences. Playing this game helped Ananya understand the rationale behind rules and consequences, and Meera and Rajesh saw the importance of consistency in their discipline approach.

Key Tips: Ensure the game reflects real-life scenarios and consequences to make it relevant. Involve children in creating the game to increase engagement.

Lifestyle Choices

Conflict: Aarav's preference for junk food clashed with Meera's emphasis on healthy eating. **Activity:** Healthy Lifestyle Challenge **Story:** The family embarked on a "Healthy Lifestyle Challenge," where they tracked their eating habits, exercised together, and celebrated each small victory. This collective effort made Aarav more conscious of his choices and brought the family closer.

Key Tips: Set achievable challenges and provide diverse options to cater to individual preferences. Celebrate collective achievements to foster a sense of team spirit.

Personality Clashes

Conflict: Rajesh's strict nature often clashed with Ananya's free-spirited personality. **Activity:** Strengths Spotlight **Story:** Every Sunday, the family dedicated time to highlight each other's strengths. Rajesh appreciated Ananya's creativity in art, and Ananya valued Rajesh's problem-solving skills. This mutual appreciation reduced their conflicts significantly.

Key Tips: Ensure every family member has an equal opportunity to showcase their strengths. Provide positive feedback and reinforcement to build self-esteem.

External Stressors

Conflict: Financial strain from Rajesh's work affected family harmony. **Activity:** Stress Relief Toolkit Creation **Story:** One weekend, the Sharma's created a "Stress Relief Toolkit" with activities like meditation, yoga, and art. These shared activities helped them manage stress and brought a sense of unity and support within the family.

Key Tips: Include a variety of stress-relief techniques to accommodate different preferences. Regularly update the toolkit to keep it effective and engaging.

Privacy and Independence

Conflict: Ananya's need for privacy often conflicted with her parents' concerns about safety. **Activity:** Independence Milestones Celebration **Story:** To balance privacy and safety, the Sharma's celebrated milestones that marked Ananya's growing independence, such as getting her first mobile phone with guidelines for responsible use. This celebration acknowledged her maturity and fostered trust.

Key Tips: Clearly define what constitutes a milestone to avoid ambiguity. Ensure rewards are meaningful and aligned with the child's interests.

Peer Influence

Conflict: Rajesh was concerned about Aarav's new friends and their influence. **Activity:** Peer Pressure Role-play **Story:** The family engaged in role-playing scenarios to prepare Aarav for peer pressure situations. This exercise not only equipped Aarav with strategies to handle negative influences but also reassured Rajesh about his son's ability to make sound decisions.

Key Tips: Discuss real-life peer pressure scenarios to keep role-plays relevant. Follow up with discussions on feelings and choices made during role-plays.

Technology and Social Media

Conflict: Disputes over screen time and appropriate online content were common. **Activity:** Digital Detox and Family Game Night **Story:** The Sharma's instituted a weekly "Digital Detox," replacing screen time with board games and outdoor activities. This not only reduced conflicts over technology but also strengthened their family bond through shared, screen-free experiences.

Key Tips: Establish clear guidelines for the digital detox period. Choose games and activities that cater to the interests of all family members to ensure full participation.

Conclusion

Through creativity, open communication, and mutual respect, the Sharma family transformed their conflicts into opportunities for growth and connection. By embracing activity-based solutions and valuing each member's perspective, they navigated the tides of change with resilience and love, setting a powerful example for families everywhere.

Understanding for Parent-Child Conflicts

1. Developmental Changes

- **Conflict:** The transition into adolescence brings about a natural desire for greater independence, which can clash with parental rules and expectations, particularly in areas such as curfews, social interactions, and personal expression.

- **Key Tips:** Implement regular check-ins to openly discuss and adjust expectations. Encourage the child's independence in decision-making within clearly defined boundaries to foster responsibility and self-confidence.

2. Differing Expectations

- **Conflict:** Disagreements often arise from misaligned expectations regarding academic performance, household responsibilities, and future goals. These conflicts can stem from a lack of clear communication about what is expected and why.
- **Key Tips:** Employ SMART criteria (Specific, Measurable, Achievable, Relevant, Time-bound) when setting expectations. Celebrate effort and progress to reinforce motivation and self-esteem, rather than focusing solely on final outcomes.

3. Communication Styles

- **Conflict:** Differences in communication styles can lead to misunderstandings and frustrations. Parents might prefer a more directive approach, while children, especially teenagers, may seek a more collaborative communication style.
- **Key Tips:** Utilize "I feel... when... because..." statements to facilitate expressing emotions and needs without casting blame. Establish a dedicated "safe space" and time for family discussions, ensuring a setting where all members feel comfortable and valued.

4. Discipline and Behavior Management

- **Conflict:** Conflicts over discipline often arise from inconsistencies in enforcement or perceptions of unfairness. Children and adolescents may resist rules they see as arbitrary or overly punitive.
- **Key Tips:** Implement a "cool-off" period for both parties before discussing misbehaviors to prevent heated arguments. Involve the child in the process of setting rules and consequences to increase their sense of ownership and responsibility.

5. Lifestyle Choices

- **Conflict:** Divergences in lifestyle choices, such as dietary habits, leisure activities, and time management, can become contentious issues, reflecting deeper differences in values and priorities.
- **Key Tips:** Model healthy lifestyle choices to set a positive example. Provide informed options rather than dictating choices, encouraging the child to make decisions that reflect both personal preferences and healthy practices.

6. Personality Clashes

- **Conflict:** Natural differences in temperament and personality between parents and children can lead to ongoing tensions, with each party feeling misunderstood or undervalued.
- **Key Tips:** Regularly acknowledge and praise each other's positive traits and strengths. Engage in cooperative activities that require teamwork, leveraging each other's strengths to achieve common goals.

7. External Stressors

- **Conflict:** Stressors external to the immediate family dynamic, such as financial strain, work pressures, or academic challenges, can exacerbate tensions within the family, leading to increased conflict.
- **Key Tips:** Create and maintain family rituals that offer stability and comfort. Practice and encourage stress-relief techniques such as mindfulness, physical activity, or shared hobbies to manage stress collectively.

8. Privacy and Independence

- **Conflict:** Navigating the balance between respecting a child's growing need for privacy and ensuring their safety and well-being can be challenging, leading to conflicts over issues like social media usage, time spent with friends, and personal space.
- **Key Tips:** Clearly define and communicate what information is considered private and what needs to be shared for safety reasons.

Incrementally increase privileges and freedoms as the child demonstrates responsible and trustworthy behavior.

9. Peer Influence

- **Conflict:** Parents may worry about the influence of their child's peer group, particularly if they believe these peers encourage negative behaviors. This can lead to conflicts over the child's choice of friends and activities.

- **Key Tips:** Role-play scenarios involving peer pressure to help the child develop effective responses. Encourage participation in extracurricular activities to broaden the child's social circle and expose them to a variety of positive influences.

10. Technology and Social Media

- **Conflict:** The digital age has introduced conflicts over screen time, internet safety, and the appropriateness of content, with parents and children often having divergent views on these issues.

- **Key Tips:** Develop a family media plan that includes designated screen-free times and areas within the home to encourage offline activities and interactions. Stay informed about the latest trends in digital media and online safety to guide and educate the child effectively.

Incorporating these expanded insights and practical tips into daily life can significantly enhance the parent-child relationship. It's important to approach conflicts not merely as obstacles but as opportunities for growth, understanding, and strengthening the family bond. Open communication, empathy, flexibility, and mutual respect are key principles in navigating these challenges successfully.

Creative solutions for resolving Parent-Child Conflicts

Activity-based technique, can expand on the comprehensive strategy for addressing parent-child relationship challenges:

1. Developmental Changes

- **Conflict:** Adolescents' quest for independence may clash with parental authority.
- **Activity:** Goal-setting Workshop - Collaboratively create a vision board or set of goals reflecting the child's aspirations, incorporating steps for gradually increasing responsibilities and freedoms.
- **Importance:** Acknowledges the child's growing autonomy and aligns parental support with the child's evolving needs, fostering independence within a supportive framework.
- **Key Tips:** Ensure goals are realistic and achievable to maintain motivation. Celebrate each achieved milestone to reinforce positive development.

2. Differing Expectations

- **Conflict:** Conflicts arise from differing views on responsibilities and achievements.
- **Activity:** Family Contract - Draft a "family contract" that outlines mutual expectations, responsibilities, and consequences, ensuring everyone's voice is heard.
- **Importance:** Clarifies and formalizes expectations, promoting mutual respect and accountability through a tangible agreement.
- **Key Tips:** Review and revise the contract periodically to reflect changes in circumstances or expectations. Use positive language to frame responsibilities and consequences.

3. Communication Styles

- **Conflict:** Misunderstandings due to differences in communication styles.
- **Activity:** Role-reversal Exercise - Take turns playing each other's roles to express and address common issues, fostering empathy and understanding.

- **Importance:** Enhances empathy by allowing family members to experience and understand each other's perspectives, improving communication and reducing conflicts.

- **Key Tips:** Encourage honest expression during role-play without judgment. Discuss the insights gained from the experience to enhance understanding.

4. Discipline and Behavior Management

- **Conflict:** Disagreements over discipline strategies and fairness.

- **Activity:** Problem-solving Board Game - Design a game that involves navigating challenges with various choices and consequences.

- **Importance:** Teaches the consequences of actions in a fun way, encouraging critical thinking and responsible decision-making.

- **Key Tips:** Ensure the game reflects real-life scenarios and consequences to make it relevant. Involve children in creating the game to increase engagement.

5. Lifestyle Choices

- **Conflict:** Disagreements over health habits, leisure activities, and time management.

- **Activity:** Healthy Lifestyle Challenge - Initiate a challenge involving healthy eating, exercise, and wellness activities, with shared tracking and celebrations.

- **Importance:** Promotes healthy choices through positive reinforcement and shared experiences, highlighting the benefits of healthy decisions.

- **Key Tips:** Set achievable challenges and provide diverse options to cater to individual preferences. Celebrate collective achievements to foster a sense of team spirit.

6. Personality Clashes

- **Conflict:** Natural personality differences lead to ongoing friction.

- Activity: Strengths Spotlight - Regularly showcase individual talents or strengths, followed by group activities that leverage each person's abilities.

- **Importance:** Promotes appreciation for each other's unique traits, reducing personality-based conflicts by focusing on strengths.

- **Key Tips:** Ensure every family member has an equal opportunity to showcase their strengths. Provide positive feedback and reinforcement to build self-esteem.

7. External Stressors

- **Conflict:** External pressures exacerbate family tensions.

- **Activity:** Stress Relief Toolkit Creation - Collaboratively create a toolkit with activities, games, and techniques for stress reduction.

- **Importance:** Provides practical tools for managing stress and fosters open discussions about handling external pressures healthily.

- **Key Tips:** Include a variety of stress-relief techniques to accommodate different preferences. Regularly update the toolkit to keep it effective and engaging.

8. Privacy and Independence

- **Conflict:** Balancing the child's desire for privacy with parental concerns.

- **Activity:** Independence Milestones Celebration - Mark key milestones towards independence, celebrating achievements with family ceremonies or rewards.

- **Importance:** Acknowledges and rewards steps towards independence, reinforcing responsible behavior and trust.

- **Key Tips:** Clearly define what constitutes a milestone to avoid ambiguity. Ensure rewards are meaningful and aligned with the child's interests.

9. Peer Influence

- **Conflict:** Concerns over the child's peer group and their influence.
- **Activity:** Peer Pressure Role-play - Engage in role-play scenarios involving peer pressure to discuss and practice constructive responses.
- **Importance:** Prepares children for real-life situations involving peer pressure, equipping them with strategies to maintain integrity and make positive choices.
- **Key Tips:** Discuss real-life peer pressure scenarios to keep role-plays relevant. Follow up with discussions on feelings and choices made during role-plays.

10. Technology and Social Media

- **Conflict:** Disputes over digital device usage and online content.
- **Activity:** Digital Detox and Family Game Night - Schedule regular periods where all family members disconnect from technology to engage in traditional games or outdoor activities.
- **Importance:** Emphasizes the value of face-to-face interactions and shared experiences, encouraging a healthy balance between digital and real-world activities.
- **Key Tips:** Establish clear guidelines for the digital detox period. Choose games and activities that cater to the interests of all family members to ensure full participation.

By integrating these detailed strategies, activities, and key tips into the family routine, parents and children can work together to address conflicts constructively, enhancing their relationship through shared experiences and open communication. These activities not only aim to resolve specific issues but also to strengthen the family unit, making it more resilient in the face of challenges.

AI / ChatGPT-Enhanced Parenting for Balanced Child Growth

Story: Nina's New Learning Companion

Introduction

In a quaint town in India, there lived a little girl named Nina. Nina was curious about everything around her, always asking questions and seeking new adventures. Her parents, Priya and Raj, wanted to nurture her curiosity and support her growth. One day, Raj came across an article about using artificial intelligence, specifically ChatGPT, to enhance children's learning and development. Intrigued, he decided to introduce Nina to this new, interactive way of learning.

The Story

Nina's adventures with ChatGPT began on a sunny morning. Priya and Raj set clear boundaries for her screen time and decided to engage with her during these interactions to ensure content appropriateness. They explained that ChatGPT was a tool to help her learn and explore new things, but it was important to balance this with other activities.

Educational Content and Language Development

One evening, as Nina was playing with her dolls, she asked, "Papa, can you tell me a story about a brave princess?" Raj smiled and suggested, "Why don't we ask ChatGPT for a story?" Nina's eyes lit up with excitement. Together, they asked ChatGPT to generate a story about a brave princess who saved her kingdom. As they listened to the story, Nina's imagination soared, and her language skills improved as she learned new words and phrases.

Another day, Nina struggled with her homework. She had to learn about shapes and colours. Priya suggested using ChatGPT to explain these concepts in a fun way. Nina was thrilled to play a game where ChatGPT described shapes and colours, and she had to find objects around the house that matched the descriptions. This interactive learning made her homework enjoyable and effective.

Responsible Digital Interaction and Emotional Intelligence

Priya and Raj also wanted to teach Nina about digital literacy. They explained that interacting with ChatGPT could help her learn how to use digital tools responsibly. Under their supervision, Nina learned the basics of digital communication and understood the importance of using technology wisely.

One afternoon, Nina was feeling upset because her friend had taken her favourite toy. Priya used ChatGPT to discuss emotions and feelings through a story about two friends who resolved their conflict. This helped Nina recognize and name her emotions, fostering her emotional intelligence. ChatGPT also presented simple problems within the story, guiding Nina to think of solutions and develop empathy.

Creativity and Imagination

To nurture Nina's creativity, Priya and Raj used ChatGPT to offer creative prompts for drawing and crafting. ChatGPT suggested, "Why don't you draw a picture of the brave princess from our story?" Nina eagerly picked up her crayons and brought the princess to life on paper. They also created imaginative scenarios for pretend play, which boosted Nina's cognitive and social development.

Routine and Habits

ChatGPT helped reinforce healthy habits and routines. It narrated engaging stories about the importance of brushing teeth, eating vegetables, and following a bedtime routine. Through these stories, Nina learned the value of daily routines and responsibilities. She even started helping her parents with small chores, understanding the importance of contributing to family life.

Interactive Learning and Problem-Solving Skills

ChatGPT became Nina's companion in interactive learning. It engaged her in conversations about her interests, from dinosaurs to space, making learning more appealing than passive video content. For homework assistance, ChatGPT provided explanations in an interactive way, making learning enjoyable.

ChatGPT also presented interactive puzzles, riddles, and math problems, encouraging Nina to think critically and solve problems. Language games and activities, like building sentences and learning new words, made learning dynamic and engaging.

Physical Activity Promotion and Family Bonding

To promote physical activity, ChatGPT suggested simple indoor exercises and physical activities, encouraging Nina to take breaks from the screen and engage in physical play. It also provided ideas for family game nights and educational discussions, fostering family bonding without screens.

Flip Side of the Concept

While ChatGPT enhanced Nina's learning experience, Priya and Raj were mindful of the potential drawbacks. They noticed that Nina sometimes preferred interacting with ChatGPT over playing outside with friends. They realized the importance of balancing screen time with outdoor play, social interactions, and hands-on learning. They set strict time limits for ChatGPT interactions and ensured Nina engaged in diverse activities.

Key Takeaways

1. **Balanced Use of Technology:** Integrating AI like ChatGPT into parenting can enrich a child's learning, but it's crucial to balance screen time with other activities.

2. **Active Supervision:** Parents should actively engage with their children during ChatGPT interactions to guide conversations and ensure content appropriateness.

3. **Holistic Growth:** ChatGPT can support educational content, language development, emotional intelligence, creativity, and routine, but it should complement physical, social, and emotional development.

4. **Diverse Activities:** Encourage a variety of activities, including outdoor play, reading, and hands-on learning, to provide a well-rounded experience for children.

Conclusion

Nina's journey with ChatGPT illustrated the potential of AI in enhancing children's growth. With careful supervision and balanced use, Priya and Raj provided Nina with a rich, interactive, and holistic learning experience. Their story serves as an inspiration for parents to embrace technology thoughtfully, ensuring it complements their child's overall development.

AI / ChatGPT-Enhanced Parenting for Balanced Child Growth

"AI/ChatGPT-Enhanced Parenting for Balanced Child Growth" encapsulates the concept of utilizing artificial intelligence, specifically ChatGPT, as a tool in the parenting process to support and enrich a child's development across various domains.

This approach integrates AI into educational activities, creative play, and emotional learning, aiming to achieve a balanced and holistic growth for children.

It emphasizes the careful and supervised use of technology to enhance learning experiences, promote healthy screen time habits, and foster overall well-being in children, ensuring that their engagement with AI complements their physical, social, and emotional development

ChatGPT can be a helpful tool for parents in the early childhood parenting process, especially when used under their guidance. Here are several ways ChatGPT can assist:

2. Educational Content

- **Storytelling:** Generate age-appropriate stories with moral lessons or fun adventures to enhance the child's imagination and language skills.
- **Basic Concepts:** Explain simple concepts in a fun and engaging way, such as colors, shapes, numbers, and letters, to support early learning.

3. Language Development

- **Language Games:** Create simple language games to help children improve their vocabulary and grammar in an interactive and playful manner.
- **Question-Answer Sessions:** Encourage children to ask questions about the world around them, and provide age-appropriate explanations to satisfy their curiosity.

4. **Responsible Digital Interaction**
- **Digital Literacy:** Interacting with ChatGPT under supervision can help children learn how to use digital tools responsibly and understand the basics of digital communication.

5. **Emotional Intelligence**
- **Emotion Recognition:** Discuss emotions and feelings through stories or hypothetical scenarios, helping children to recognize and name their own emotions.
- **Problem-Solving Skills:** Present simple problems or conflicts within stories and guide the child to think of solutions, fostering critical thinking and empathy.

6. **Creativity and Imagination**
- **Creative Prompts:** Offer creative prompts for drawing, crafting, or storytelling activities that parents and children can do together.
- **Imaginative Scenarios:** Create imaginative scenarios for pretend play, which is vital for cognitive and social development.

7. **Routine and Habits**
- **Healthy Habits:** Discuss the importance of daily routines and healthy habits like brushing teeth, eating vegetables, and bedtime routines through engaging narratives.
- **Responsibility:** Introduce concepts of small chores or responsibilities suitable for their age to teach them about contributing to family life.

Using ChatGPT as an alternative to traditional mobile device usage for kids involves leveraging its interactive and educational capabilities to engage children in more productive and enriching activities. Here's how ChatGPT can help in this regard:

1. Interactive Learning

- **Educational Dialogue:** Engage children in conversations about their interests, such as dinosaurs, space, or history, providing informative and engaging content that can replace passive screen time.

- **Homework Assistance:** Use ChatGPT to help with homework questions, offering explanations in an interactive way that can make learning more appealing than passive video content.

2. Creative Engagement

- **Storytelling and Writing:** Encourage children to write stories or poems with ChatGPT, which can help them in brainstorming ideas, creating storylines, or developing characters, making the creative process interactive and fun.

- **Art and Music:** ChatGPT can suggest DIY art projects, explain art techniques, or even help in composing simple songs or music, fostering creativity without the need for constant screen interaction.

3. Problem-Solving Skills

- **Interactive Puzzles and Riddles:** Present children with puzzles, riddles, or math problems that ChatGPT can generate, encouraging them to think critically and solve problems interactively.

- **Language Games:** Use language-based games and activities, like building sentences, learning new words, or language puzzles, to make learning more dynamic and engaging.

4. Physical Activity Promotion

- **Activity Ideas:** ChatGPT can suggest physical activities or simple indoor exercises for kids, encouraging them to take breaks from the screen and engage in physical play or family activities.

5. Mindfulness and Emotional Well-being

- **Mindfulness Exercises:** Use ChatGPT to guide children through simple mindfulness or breathing exercises, promoting emotional regulation and providing a calming alternative to screen time.

- **Emotional Support Conversations**: ChatGPT can engage in simple, supportive conversations that help children express their feelings and learn about emotional health in an age-appropriate way.

6. Family Bonding

- **Family Game Nights:** ChatGPT can provide ideas for family board games, quizzes, or interactive storytelling sessions, encouraging family time without screens.

- **Educational Discussions:** Use ChatGPT to spark family discussions on a variety of topics, from science to literature, promoting a culture of learning and curiosity.

Implementation Tips

- **Set Clear Boundaries:** Establish specific times and durations for ChatGPT interaction, ensuring it doesn't lead to excessive screen time.

- **Active Supervision:** Parents should actively engage with their children during ChatGPT interactions to guide the conversation and ensure content appropriateness.

- **Encourage Diverse Activities:** Balance ChatGPT interactions with a variety of other activities, including outdoor play, reading, and hands-on learning, to provide a well-rounded experience for children.

Adolescence Bliss Excursion

Adolescence Bliss Excursion

What? - "Adolescence"

Adolescence / teenage typically encompasses the ages of 10 to 19, marking the transition from childhood to adulthood.

During the adolescent stage of life, relationships play a crucial role in shaping an individual's development and well-being.

Adolescents form relationships with peers, family members, and mentors, which impact their self-esteem, identity formation, and ability to navigate the challenges of this transitional period.

Positive relationships provide support, a sense of belonging, and opportunities for learning important social skills, fostering resilience and overall mental health.

Why? - Significance of "Bliss"

At adolescent stage of life, relationships play a crucial role in shaping an individual's development and well-being. These connections contribute to emotional, social, and cognitive growth. Adolescents form relationships with peers, family members, and mentors, which impact their self-esteem, identity formation, and ability to navigate the challenges of this transitional period.

How? "Adolescence Bliss Excursion"

Nature and activity-based teen bliss excursion" is a wellbeing approach that emphasizes engaging teenagers in outdoor activities, exploring nature, and incorporating hands-on experiences into their learning and development.

This type of excursion involves taking teenagers outside of their usual environment to participate in activities that foster a connection with nature and promote physical, cognitive, and social development.

Trips to nature reserves, or other outdoor spaces where they can explore, play, and learn from their surroundings.

The activities planned during these excursions are often designed to be interactive, allowing them to engage with the natural world and develop various skills while having fun.

This aims to provide a holistic learning experience, incorporating elements of environmental education, physical activity, and social interaction to support their overall growth and well-being

Road Map for Adolescence Bliss Excursion:

We strive to make adolescence bliss easier and more enjoyable via following activity-based modules, in the lap of nature, through our Professionals design activities, keeping all psychological and scientific factors in mind.

Challenges Faced by Today's Teenagers & Means to Overcoming it

Story: "Finding Balance in Nature: A Journey of Overcoming Teen Challenges"

In the bustling city of Pune, lived a teenager named Aanya. At 16, she was navigating the intricate maze of adolescence, juggling schoolwork, friendships, and personal struggles. Aanya's life was a whirlwind of academic pressure, social media, and mounting expectations. Her parents, Rohan and Meera, noticed her growing anxiety and decided it was time for a change.

One weekend, they proposed a family trip to the Western Ghats, a place where they had spent their own childhood summers. Reluctant at first, Aanya agreed, hoping to escape the stress that seemed to shadow her every move.

As they reached the serene hills, Aanya's initial apprehension melted away. The fresh air, the lush greenery, and the soothing sounds of nature had a calming effect on her restless mind. Rohan and Meera had planned a series of nature-based activities to help Aanya reconnect with herself and her surroundings.

Mental Health Issues:

On the first morning, they embarked on a gentle hike through the forest. The rhythmic crunch of leaves underfoot and the melodies of birds lifted Aanya's spirits. She felt her anxiety ebb away, replaced by a sense of peace she hadn't felt in months.

Academic Pressure:

During their hike, they found a quiet clearing where they set up a study session. With the sun filtering through the trees and a gentle breeze providing a comforting backdrop, Aanya found it easier to concentrate. The natural environment sparked her creativity, making her schoolwork feel less like a burden and more like an enjoyable challenge.

Social Pressures and Bullying:

The following day, the family joined a group of fellow campers for a team-building exercise. Navigating an obstacle course in the woods, Aanya learned to communicate and collaborate with others. The shared experience fostered new friendships and boosted her confidence, helping her realize the importance of positive relationships.

Screen Addiction and Technology Overload:

Rohan declared a "digital detox" day. Initially resistant, Aanya soon found joy in rediscovering old hobbies. She spent the day sketching the landscape, practicing mindfulness, and simply being present. The absence of screens allowed her to reconnect with herself and her surroundings, rejuvenating her mind.

Social Isolation:

Aanya's parents encouraged her to participate in a community gardening project nearby. Working alongside locals, Aanya felt a sense of belonging and purpose. The act of nurturing plants and seeing them thrive mirrored her own journey of growth and healing.

Body Image and Self-Esteem Issues:

One morning, they practiced yoga on a hilltop. Surrounded by nature, Aanya felt a deep connection to her body. The practice wasn't about appearance but about embracing the strength and grace of her movements. This newfound appreciation for her body boosted her self-esteem and fostered a healthier self-image.

Lack of Physical Activity:

Each day was filled with activities like biking and kayaking. The physical exertion in such beautiful surroundings was invigorating. Aanya realized that exercise could be fun and fulfilling, not just a chore.

Family and Peer Relationships:

The trip culminated in a family picnic by a tranquil lake. As they shared stories and laughter, Aanya felt a renewed bond with her parents. The neutral, positive environment of nature allowed them to communicate openly and strengthen their relationship.

Back in Pune, Aanya carried these lessons with her. She continued to integrate nature into her daily life, whether through morning walks, outdoor study sessions, or weekend hikes. Her parents, too, made it a point to plan regular family outings in nature, fostering their bond and supporting Aanya's growth.

Aanya's journey through nature taught her that while challenges are inevitable, they can be overcome with the right support and environment. Nature became her sanctuary, a place where she found balance, resilience, and a deeper connection to herself and her loved ones.

Challenges faced by today's Teenagers & means to Overcoming it

Teenagers today face a variety of challenges that can impact their physical, emotional, and mental well-being. Nature-based activities can offer a holistic approach to overcoming these challenges.

1. **Mental Health Issues:**
- **Nature-Based Activity:** Engaging in outdoor activities like hiking, camping, or simply spending time in natural settings.
- **Advantages:** Nature has a calming effect, reduces stress, and promotes overall well-being.
- **Tips:** Encourage regular outdoor breaks, practice mindfulness in nature, and foster a connection with the environment.

2. **Academic Pressure:**
- **Nature-Based Activity:** Outdoor study sessions or group activities in natural surroundings.
- **Advantages:** Nature enhances creativity and cognitive function, providing a refreshing break from academic stress.
- **Tips:** Create nature-friendly study environments, explore educational trails, and organize study groups in parks.

3. **Social Pressures and Bullying:**
- **Nature-Based Activity:** Group outdoor adventures or team-building activities in natural settings.
- **Advantages:** Nature fosters teamwork, communication, and a sense of community, helping teens build positive relationships.
- **Tips:** Organize nature-based group activities, promote inclusivity, and facilitate open communication.

4. **Screen Addiction and Technology Overload:**
- **Nature-Based Activity:** Digital detox days spent outdoors, away from screens.

- **Advantages:** Disconnecting from technology in nature improves focus, reduces eye strain, and promotes physical activity.
- **Tips:** Plan device-free outings, encourage hobbies that involve nature, and set screen time limits.

5. **Social Isolation:**
- **Nature-based Activity:** Community gardening or volunteering in outdoor projects.
- **Importance:** Participating in nature-based community activities fosters social connections and a sense of belonging.
- **Tips:** Encourage involvement in environmental or community service organizations, where shared goals can create meaningful connections.

6. **Body Image and Self-Esteem Issues:**
- **Nature-Based Activity:** Outdoor physical activities like hiking, biking, or yoga.
- **Advantages:** Nature promotes body positivity, boosts self-esteem, and encourages a healthier relationship with one's body.
- **Tips:** Emphasize the joy of movement, focus on overall well-being rather than appearance, and celebrate achievements in outdoor activities.

7. **Lack of Physical Activity:**
- **Nature-based Activity:** Outdoor sports, such as biking, hiking, or kayaking.
- **Importance:** Regular physical activity in nature promotes fitness, boosts mood, and helps combat sedentary habits.
- **Tips:** Find local outdoor recreation options, encourage participation in sports teams, and make family outings cantered around physical activities in nature.

8. **Family and Peer Relationships:**

- **Nature-Based Activity:** Family hikes, picnics, or outdoor team-building activities with peers.

- **Advantages:** Nature provides a neutral and positive environment for fostering family and peer relationships.

- **Tips:** Plan regular nature outings with family and friends, encourage open communication, and build a support system.

It's important to note that while nature-based activities can be beneficial, they may not be a one-size-fits-all solution. Individual preferences and circumstances vary, so a combination of approaches may be needed to address the specific challenges faced by each teenager. Additionally, fostering a supportive and understanding environment is crucial in helping teenagers overcome these challenges.

Adolescent Affiliation & Relationship Issues: Key Area of Realization

Story: The Journey to Heartfelt Connections

Characters:

- **Arjun:** A 16-year-old boy who is struggling with various relationship issues.

- **Neha:** Arjun's 14-year-old sister who also faces her own set of adolescent challenges.
- **Ravi:** Their father, who believes in the power of nature-based activities to solve problems.
- **Meera:** Their mother, who supports the family with her nurturing and empathetic approach.

Setting:

A picturesque village in the foothills of the Himalayas, surrounded by lush forests, serene lakes, and open meadows.

Arjun was in his teenage years, a time filled with confusion and change. He often felt misunderstood, especially when it came to his friends and family. One day, after a heated argument with his best friend over a trivial issue, he decided to confide in his father, Ravi, who had always been a source of wisdom.

Communication Challenges "Dad, why is it so hard to talk to people?" Arjun asked.

Ravi smiled and suggested they go on a hike the next morning. As they walked through the forest, Ravi encouraged Arjun to express his feelings openly. The fresh air and the rhythmic sound of their footsteps created a perfect environment for heartfelt conversations. Arjun realized the importance of effective communication and active listening.

Peer Pressure Meanwhile, Neha was struggling with peer pressure. She felt the need to fit in and often found herself making choices she wasn't comfortable with. One weekend, Ravi organized a team sports event with local kids. The games were fun and challenging, and Neha discovered a sense of belonging without succumbing to negative influences. She learned to distinguish between positive and negative peer pressure and developed the confidence to make independent choices.

Conflict Resolution Back at school, Arjun faced conflicts with his classmates. Understanding that disagreements are natural, Ravi took Arjun and his friends to a ropes course. The collaborative tasks required them to work together, communicate, and resolve conflicts constructively. Arjun learned valuable conflict resolution skills and understood that differences could be managed positively.

Identity and Self-Esteem Issues Neha often felt insecure about her identity and self-worth. One peaceful evening, Ravi took her on a solitary hike. The tranquillity of nature provided Neha with the space for introspection and self-reflection. As she journaled her thoughts in the serene environment, she realized the importance of self-acceptance and that everyone goes through a process of self-discovery.

Dating and Relationship Boundaries Arjun was beginning to explore romantic relationships and found it challenging to communicate his boundaries. Ravi suggested a relaxed nature walk with his friend. The calm setting of a forest trail allowed them to have open conversations about expectations and boundaries, helping Arjun understand the importance of clear communication in relationships.

Trust and Betrayal Arjun had experienced betrayal by a close friend, which made him wary of trusting others. To rebuild his sense of trust, Ravi involved Arjun in a community garden project. Working together towards a common goal fostered trust and teamwork, showing Arjun the significance of trust in relationships.

Jealousy and Insecurity Neha often felt jealous and insecure among her friends. Ravi encouraged her to engage in solo hikes and nature journaling. These activities promoted self-discovery and self-esteem, helping Neha understand that jealousy often stemmed from personal insecurities.

Social media and Technology Impact Both Arjun and Neha were heavily influenced by social media, impacting their relationships. Ravi planned a family camping trip with a digital detox. Spending time in nature, away from screens, allowed them to connect more deeply with each other and understand the importance of balancing online and offline interactions.

Digital Dependency Recognizing the need for face-to-face interactions, Ravi organized "unplugged" outdoor adventures, like picnics and beach days. These activities encouraged real-time connections without digital distractions, helping Arjun and Neha reduce their dependence on social media for validation.

Parent-Teen Relationships Arjun often felt distant from his parents. Ravi and Meera decided to engage in gardening together. The relaxed atmosphere of working with plants created opportunities for open conversations and bonding. They realized the importance of communication, empathy, and mutual respect in their relationships.

Time Management Balancing relationships with responsibilities was a challenge for both siblings. Ravi encouraged them to participate in community clean-up projects. These activities required planning and time management, teaching them how to balance their time effectively.

Through these nature-based activities, Arjun and Neha discovered the therapeutic and calming power of the outdoors. They experienced personal growth, built healthier relationships, and gained new perspectives on life. With the guidance of their parents and the support of nature, they learned to navigate the complexities of adolescence with resilience and confidence.

Key Takeaways:

1. Effective communication is crucial for healthy relationships.

2. Positive peer pressure can build confidence, while negative peer pressure should be resisted.

3. Constructive conflict resolution strengthens bonds.

4. Self-acceptance and self-discovery are essential for personal growth.

5. Clear communication about personal boundaries fosters respectful relationships.

6. Trust is the foundation of strong relationships.

7. Building self-esteem can mitigate jealousy and insecurity.

8. Balancing online and offline interactions promotes healthier relationships.

9. Face-to-face interactions are vital for genuine connections.

10. Parent-teen relationships thrive on communication, empathy, and respect.

11. Managing time effectively ensures a balanced life.

Adolescent Affiliation & Relationship Issues: Key area of Realization

Teenagers and adolescents often face a variety of relationship problems as they navigate the complexities of social interactions and personal development. Here are some common issues, key areas of realization, and nature-based activities that can help address these problems:

1. **Communication Challenges:**
- **Key Area of Realization:** Understanding the importance of effective communication, active listening, and expressing feelings openly.
- **Nature-Based Activity:** Engaging in activities like hiking or camping where individuals can talk freely without distractions can improve communication skills and strengthen connections.

2. **Peer Pressure:**
- **Key Area of Realization:** Recognizing the difference between positive and negative peer pressure, and developing the confidence to make independent choices.
- **Nature-Based Activity:** Group activities like team sports or adventure challenges can foster a sense of belonging without succumbing to negative influences.

3. **Conflict Resolution:**
- **Key Area of Realization:** Learning to manage conflicts constructively and understanding that disagreements are a natural part of relationships.

- **Nature-Based Activity:** Participating in outdoor team-building activities, such as ropes courses or collaborative projects, can promote teamwork and conflict resolution skills.

4. **Identity and Self-Esteem Issues:**
- **Key Area of Realization:** Realizing the importance of self-acceptance and understanding that everyone goes through a process of self-discovery.
- **Nature-Based Activity:** Spending time alone in nature, like hiking or journaling in a peaceful outdoor setting, can provide space for introspection and self-reflection.

5. **Dating and Relationship Boundaries:**
- **Key Area of Realization:** Recognizing the need for clear communication about personal boundaries and respecting the boundaries of others.
- **Nature-Based Activity:** Going on a relaxed nature walk or picnic can provide a comfortable environment for open conversations about expectations and boundaries in relationships.

6. **Trust and Betrayal:**
- **Realization:** Learning the significance of trust in relationships and understanding the consequences of betrayal.
- **Nature-Based Activity:** Collaborate on projects like building a community garden or maintaining a nature trail, fostering trust and teamwork through shared responsibilities.

7. **Jealousy and Insecurity:**
- **Realization:** Understanding that jealousy often stems from personal insecurities and the importance of building self-confidence.
- **Nature-Based Activity:** Engaging in activities that promote self-discovery and self-esteem, such as solo hikes, nature journaling, or meditation in a natural setting.

8. **Social Media and Technology Impact:**
- **Key Area of Realization:** Understanding the influence of social media on relationships and establishing a healthy balance between online and offline interactions.
- **Nature-Based Activity:** Taking a digital detox and spending time in nature, like camping or simply enjoying a day at the beach, can help reduce the impact of technology on relationships.

9. **Digital Dependency:**
- **Realization:** Understanding the need for face-to-face interactions and reducing dependence on social media for validation.
- **Nature-Based Activity:** Plan "unplugged" outdoor adventures, like a day at the beach or a picnic in the park, to encourage real-time connections without digital distractions.

10. **Parent-Teen Relationships:**
- **Key Area of Realization:** Acknowledging the importance of communication, empathy, and mutual respect in parent-teen relationships.
- **Nature-Based Activity:** Engaging in activities like gardening or nature walks together can create a relaxed atmosphere for open conversations and bonding.

11. **Time Management:**
- **Realization:** Learning to balance relationships with other responsibilities and personal growth.
- **Nature-Based Activity:** Schedule nature-based activities that require planning and time management, such as organizing a community clean-up or participating in environmental conservation projects.

Nature-based activities can provide a therapeutic and calming environment, fostering personal growth and healthier relationships. Additionally, the outdoors offers opportunities for shared experiences, building bonds, and gaining new perspectives on life and relationships.

Additionally, seeking guidance from trusted adults, mentors, or counsellors can provide valuable support in navigating relationship challenges during adolescence.

Values for Teenagers

Story: "Nature's Classroom: Lessons of Life for Teenagers"

Respect for the Environment

In the bustling city of Bengaluru, a group of teenagers from different schools gathered for a week-long nature camp in the serene Western Ghats. Among them were Riya, a tech-savvy girl with little exposure to nature, and Aarav, an adventurous boy with a deep love for the environment.

The first day was filled with excitement as they embarked on a hike through the lush forests. Their guide, Anil, explained the importance of preserving the environment and introduced the concept of Leave No Trace principles. As they trekked, Riya noticed the beauty of the forest and the delicate balance of its ecosystem. The group also participated in a tree-planting activity, where they learned about the vital role of trees in maintaining ecological balance.

Key Takeaway: Respecting the environment helps us appreciate its beauty and understand our responsibility towards preserving it.

Resilience

On the third day, the campers faced a challenging rock-climbing activity. Aarav, with his adventurous spirit, was excited, but Riya felt anxious. The steep cliff seemed insurmountable, but with Anil's guidance, the group started climbing.

Riya struggled at first, slipping and feeling disheartened. However, Aarav encouraged her to keep going, sharing his own experiences of overcoming challenges. Slowly, Riya found her rhythm and reached the top, feeling a sense of accomplishment she had never experienced before.

Key Takeaway: Resilience is built through facing and overcoming challenges, fostering perseverance and mental toughness.

Teamwork and Collaboration

Midweek, the group was divided into teams for a community gardening project. They worked together to clear a patch of land, plant vegetables, and set up a small irrigation system. Riya and Aarav were in the same team and learned to communicate effectively, share tasks, and support each other.

The project taught them the value of collaboration and how working harmoniously with others could achieve great results. The garden they created would not only provide food but also serve as a symbol of their collective effort.

Key Takeaway: Teamwork and collaboration enhance communication skills and the ability to work towards common goals.

Mindfulness and Presence

As the week progressed, Anil introduced the campers to mindfulness practices. One morning, they gathered for a meditation session by a tranquil river. The serene environment helped them focus on their breathing and become more self-aware.

Riya, who was usually glued to her phone, found peace in the quietness of nature. She started to appreciate the present moment and realized the importance of disconnecting from digital distractions.

Key Takeaway: Mindfulness and presence enhance self-awareness, reduce stress, and promote mental well-being.

Empathy

The group participated in a wildlife conservation project, helping to clean a nearby river and build shelters for birds. Working together for a common cause, they developed empathy for the living beings around them.

Aarav shared stories of animals he had encountered and how their habitats were being destroyed by human activities. Riya felt a deep sense of responsibility and empathy towards nature and its inhabitants.

Key Takeaway: Empathy fosters positive relationships and a sense of responsibility towards the environment and community.

Gratitude

During the last evening, the campers sat around a campfire, sharing their experiences. Anil encouraged them to reflect on what they were grateful for. Riya spoke about her newfound appreciation for nature and the friends she had made. Aarav expressed gratitude for the opportunity to share his passion for the environment.

They kept gratitude journals, recording positive experiences and the beauty they encountered during the camp. This practice helped them cultivate a positive outlook on life.

Key Takeaway: Gratitude cultivates appreciation for the natural world and promotes a positive outlook.

Integrity

Throughout the camp, the teenagers engaged in ethical discussions and activities that required honesty. During team games, they learned the importance of playing fair and being honest with each other.

Riya found that being truthful not only built trust but also fostered a strong moral compass. Aarav, known for his integrity, became a role model for others, showing that honesty and authenticity were key to building strong relationships.

Key Takeaway: Integrity builds trust and promotes honesty and authenticity.

Self-Reliance

On the last day, Anil taught the campers basic survival skills, such as building a fire, cooking outdoors, and navigating using a compass. Riya, who had always depended on others, learned to rely on herself and felt a newfound sense of confidence.

Aarav, already skilled in these areas, assisted others, reinforcing his own knowledge and leadership skills. The campers left with a sense of independence and self-reliance.

Key Takeaway: Self-reliance builds confidence and independence.

Self-Discovery

The campers were given the opportunity for solo camping, spending a night alone in the wilderness. Riya, initially apprehensive, found solitude in nature to be a powerful experience. She reflected on her life, aspirations, and the person she wanted to become.

Aarav used this time to reconnect with himself and set personal goals. The experience of self-discovery in nature was transformative for both of them.

Key Takeaway: Solitude in nature provides a conducive environment for self-reflection and personal growth.

Creativity

One afternoon, the campers engaged in art and craft activities using natural materials. They created beautiful pieces of art, inspired by the surroundings. Riya discovered her love for sketching, and Aarav enjoyed crafting sculptures from twigs and leaves. The creative process allowed them to express themselves in unique ways, finding inspiration in the natural world around them.

Key Takeaway: Nature inspires creativity, allowing for unique self-expression.

Curiosity and Lifelong Learning

On the final day, the group participated in a citizen science project, exploring the local flora and fauna and collecting data for research. Their curiosity was piqued as they learned about the biodiversity of the Western Ghats.

Riya and Aarav were fascinated by the knowledge they gained and expressed a desire to continue learning about the natural world. Anil provided resources for further exploration and encouraged them to ask questions and seek knowledge.

Key Takeaway: Curiosity about the natural world encourages a love for learning and a sense of wonder.

Conclusion

As the camp came to an end, Riya and Aarav reflected on their journey. They had learned valuable life lessons through nature-based activities, developing respect for the environment, resilience, teamwork, mindfulness, empathy, gratitude, integrity, self-reliance, self-discovery, creativity, and a lifelong love for learning. Returning to their daily lives, they carried these values with them, fostering personal growth and a deeper connection to the world around them.

Key Takeaways

1. **Respect for the Environment:** Understanding the importance of preserving nature and fostering responsibility towards it.

2. **Resilience:** Building mental toughness and perseverance through overcoming challenges.

3. **Teamwork and Collaboration**: Enhancing communication and cooperation skills by working towards common goals.

4. **Mindfulness and Presence:** Promoting self-awareness and mental well-being through mindfulness practices.

5. **Empathy:** Developing a sense of responsibility and positive relationships by understanding and sharing the feelings of others.

6. **Gratitude:** Cultivating appreciation for nature and a positive outlook on life.

7. **Integrity:** Building trust and promoting honesty and authenticity.

8. **Self-Reliance:** Fostering confidence & independence through learning survival skills.

9. **Self-Discovery:** Facilitating personal growth and reflection in solitude.

10. **Creativity:** Inspiring unique self-expression through nature-based art and craft.

11. **Curiosity and Lifelong Learning:** Encouraging a love for learning and a sense of wonder about the natural world.

By engaging in these nature-based activities, teenagers can develop essential values that will guide them through life, fostering personal growth and a deeper connection to the world around them.

Values For Teenagers: Engaging in nature-based activities can provide valuable opportunities for teenagers to develop important values. Here are some key values, along with nature-based activity techniques, advantages, and tips for cultivating them:

1. **Respect for the Environment:**
- **Nature-Based Activity Technique:** Participate in outdoor activities like hiking, camping, or volunteering for environmental conservation projects.
- **Advantages:** Understanding the importance of preserving the environment, fostering a sense of responsibility towards nature.
- **Tips:** Educate teenagers about ecosystems, wildlife, and the impact of human activities. Encourage responsible practices like Leave No Trace principles.

2. **Resilience:**
   - **Nature-Based Activity Technique:** Engage in challenging outdoor activities such as rock climbing, backpacking, or survival skills.
   - **Advantages:** Builds mental toughness, perseverance, and the ability to adapt to changing circumstances.
   - **Tips:** Encourage teenagers to embrace challenges, learn from failures, and appreciate the rewards of overcoming obstacles in nature.

3. **Teamwork and Collaboration:**
   - **Nature-Based Activity Technique:** Participate in group activities like team sports, group hikes, or community gardening projects.
   - **Advantages:** Develops communication skills, cooperation, and the ability to work harmoniously with others.
   - **Tips:** Emphasize the importance of effective communication, shared goals, and mutual support within a team setting. Debrief activities to highlight teamwork lessons.

4. **Mindfulness and Presence:**
   - **Nature-Based Activity Technique:** Practice activities like meditation, yoga, or simply spending quiet time in nature.
   - **Advantages:** Enhances self-awareness, reduces stress, and promotes mental well-being.
   - **Tips:** Teach mindfulness techniques, such as focused breathing or observing nature. Encourage unplugging from digital devices during these activities.

5. **Empathy: Understand and share the feelings of others.**
   - **Nature-Based Activity Technique:** Volunteering for environmental projects or wildlife conservation. Working towards a common cause, especially one that benefits the environment or community, helps teenagers develop empathy and a sense of social responsibility.

- **Advantages:** Empathy fosters positive relationships and a sense of community. Connecting with nature helps develop empathy towards living beings, fostering a sense of responsibility for the well-being of the environment.

- **Tips:** Encourage open communication and active listening. Teach teens to consider others' perspectives and feelings.

6. **Gratitude:**
- **Nature-Based Activity Technique:** Foster gratitude through activities like nature walks, journaling, or participating in community gardening.

- **Advantages:** Cultivates appreciation for the natural world and promotes a positive outlook.

- **Tips:** Prompt teenagers to reflect on the beauty and benefits of nature. Keep a gratitude journal to record positive experiences in the outdoors.

7. **Integrity:**
- **Activity-based technique:** Engaging in ethical discussions or participating in activities that require honesty, like team games & sports.

- **Advantages:** Builds trust, fosters a strong moral compass, and promotes honesty and authenticity.

- **Tips:** Keep a personal journal to reflect on your actions, decisions, and values. Set personal goals and hold yourself accountable for sticking to them.

8. **Self-Reliance:**
- **Nature-Based Activity Technique:** Learn survival skills, outdoor cooking, or navigation techniques.

- **Advantages:** Builds confidence, independence, and the ability to rely on oneself in various situations.

- **Tips:** Start with basic skills and gradually progress to more advanced ones. Provide guidance and supervision as needed.

9. **Self-Discovery:**
- **Nature-Based Activity Technique:** Solo camping, reflective journaling in natural settings.
- **Advantages:** Solitude in nature provides a conducive environment for self-reflection and personal growth.

10. **Creativity:**
- **Nature-Based Activity Technique:** Art and craft activities using natural materials, outdoor sketching.
- **Advantages:** Nature inspires creativity, allowing teenagers to explore and express themselves in unique ways.

11. **Curiosity and Lifelong Learning:**
- **Nature-Based Activity Technique:** Explore natural environments, participate in educational nature programs, or engage in citizen science projects.
- **Advantages:** Encourages a love for learning, curiosity about the natural world, and a sense of wonder.
- **Tips:** Facilitate opportunities for hands-on exploration, encourage asking questions, and provide resources for further learning.

Encouraging teenagers to actively participate in nature-based activities can foster personal growth, character development, and a deeper connection to the world around them. Regular reflection and open communication about these experiences can enhance the impact of these values.

Life Skills for Teenagers

Story: "The Journey of Growth: An Adventure in the Western Ghats"

Story:

In a small town nestled at the foothills of the Western Ghats, a group of teenagers eagerly awaited the annual summer camp organized by their school. This year, the camp promised to be different, focusing on nature-based activities to teach essential life skills. Among the participants were

Aarav, Priya, Rohan, and Meera, each with their own set of challenges and dreams.

As the bus wound its way up the scenic hills, the excitement was palpable. The first activity was a group hike to a hidden waterfall. The journey was tough, with narrow paths and slippery rocks. The group had to communicate effectively to navigate the terrain, helping each other across obstacles. Aarav, usually shy, found himself guiding others and giving clear instructions. This experience helped him realize the importance of effective communication and active listening.

Next came an outdoor survival challenge. Divided into teams, the teens had to build shelters using materials found in the forest. Priya, who often doubted her problem-solving skills, took the lead. She encouraged her team to brainstorm and explore different approaches. Their shelter was not the best, but the debriefing session helped her understand that facing challenges and thinking critically were key to success.

The camp's highlight was a rock-climbing activity. Rohan, known for his independent streak, struggled initially. But teamwork was essential here. He learned to trust his peers, communicate, and collaborate to reach the top. This experience underscored the importance of teamwork and collaboration, teaching him that sometimes, reliance on others is crucial.

Leadership skills were honed during a wilderness survival simulation. Meera, usually a follower, was assigned the role of the group leader. She had to make decisions, delegate tasks, and ensure her team's safety. Through this, she discovered her latent leadership qualities and the value of constructive feedback.

A backpacking trip exposed the teens to changing weather conditions, teaching them resilience and adaptability. They faced rainstorms and sweltering heat, learning to stay positive and adapt to the circumstances. This experience showed them that setbacks could be valuable learning opportunities.

Critical thinking was developed through environmental exploration and wildlife observation. The teens were encouraged to ask questions and engage in discussions about the ecosystem. This nurtured their curiosity and analytical thinking.

Planning and executing a camping trip taught the importance of time management. The teens had to set up tents, cook meals, and navigate the trails. Realizing the significance of prioritizing tasks and sticking to a schedule was an eye-opener for many.

Empathy and social awareness were fostered through connecting with nature and participating in conservation projects. Understanding the interconnectedness of life and their role in preserving it helped build their social responsibility.

Overcoming outdoor challenges, like crossing a river or navigating through dense forests, boosted their self-confidence. Each successful attempt was a step towards believing in their capabilities.

Engaging in solo activities, such as solo hikes, promoted independence. These moments of solitude helped the teens reflect on their experiences and build a sense of responsibility.

Mindfulness and stress management were taught through nature walks and meditation sessions by the river. The calm and beauty of nature provided a perfect backdrop for stress relief and emotional regulation.

Finally, environmental awareness was cultivated through tree planting and wildlife observation activities. Educating them on ecological systems and the importance of conservation instilled a deep respect for the environment.

Flip Side:

However, not everything went smoothly. Some teens struggled with the physical demands, leading to frustration and conflict. A lack of proper communication at times caused misunderstandings and delays. There were moments when the challenges seemed too daunting, leading to feelings of inadequacy. But these setbacks were crucial for their growth, teaching them resilience and the importance of supporting one another.

Key Takeaways:

1. **Communication Skills:** Effective communication is essential in all aspects of life.

2. **Problem-Solving Skills:** Facing challenges independently fosters critical thinking.

3. **Teamwork and Collaboration:** Success often depends on working well with others.

4. **Leadership Skills:** Taking initiative and guiding others builds confidence.

5. **Resilience and Adaptability:** Overcoming setbacks is key to personal growth.

6. **Critical Thinking:** Curiosity and analytical thinking are vital for informed decisions.

7. **Time Management:** Prioritizing tasks and managing time are crucial for success.

8. **Empathy and Social Awareness:** Understanding and caring for others build meaningful relationships.

9. **Self-Confidence:** Confidence grows through overcoming challenges.

10. **Independence:** Being self-reliant prepares teens for adulthood.

11. **Mindfulness and Stress Management:** Nature provides a therapeutic environment for managing stress.

12. **Environmental Awareness:** Respect for the environment is essential for sustainable living.

As the camp concluded, the teenagers returned home with a newfound appreciation for nature and the life skills they had developed. The journey through the Western Ghats had not only brought them closer to nature but also to themselves, preparing them for the challenges of the future.

Life skills for teenagers

Important life skills for teenagers include a mix of personal, social, and practical skills that contribute to their overall development. Nature-based activity learning techniques can be particularly effective in fostering these skills. Here are some key life skills and tips on how they can be adopted through nature-based activities:

1. **Communication Skills:**
- **Nature-Based Activity:** Group hikes, camping trips, or team-building activities in natural settings.
- **Importance:** Effective communication is crucial in personal and professional life.
- **Tips:** Encourage group discussions, assign leadership roles, and practice active listening during nature-based activities.

2. **Problem-Solving Skills:**
- **Nature-Based Activity:** Outdoor survival challenges, navigation exercises, or building shelters.
- **Importance:** Learning to think critically and solve problems is essential for success.
- **Tips:** Allow teens to face challenges independently, encourage brainstorming, and debrief after the activity to discuss different problem-solving approaches.

3. **Teamwork and Collaboration:**
- **Nature-Based Activity:** Canoeing, rock climbing, or group environmental projects.
- **Importance:** Teamwork is vital in both personal relationships and professional settings.

- **Tips:** Emphasize the importance of each team member's role, foster a supportive environment, and encourage communication and cooperation.

4. **Leadership Skills:**
- **Nature-Based Activity:** Wilderness survival simulations, leading group hikes, or organizing outdoor events.
- **Importance:** Leadership skills empower teens to take initiative and guide others.
- **Tips:** Rotate leadership roles, provide opportunities for decision-making, and offer constructive feedback to develop leadership qualities.

5. **Resilience and Adaptability:**
- **Nature-Based Activity:** Backpacking trips, camping in changing weather conditions, or nature-based obstacle courses.
- **Importance:** Life is full of uncertainties, and resilience helps in overcoming challenges.
- **Tips:** Expose teens to varying conditions, encourage positive thinking, and discuss how setbacks can be valuable learning experiences.

6. **Critical Thinking:**
- **Nature-Based Activity:** Environmental exploration, wildlife observation, or scientific experiments in nature.
- **Importance:** Critical thinking enables teens to analyse situations and make informed decisions.
- **Tips:** Encourage curiosity, ask open-ended questions, and engage in discussions that stimulate analytical thinking.

7. **Time Management:**
- **Nature-Based Activity:** Planning and executing a camping trip, including setting up tents, cooking, and navigating.

- **Importance:** Effective time management is crucial for balancing responsibilities.
- **Tips:** Provide a schedule for activities, set realistic goals, and discuss the importance of prioritization.

8. **Empathy and Social Awareness:**
- **Nature-Based Approach:** Connecting with nature fosters a sense of empathy and social responsibility.
- **Importance:** Developing empathy helps teenagers build meaningful relationships and become socially aware citizens.

9. **Self-Confidence:**
- **Nature-Based Approach:** Overcoming outdoor challenges can boost self-confidence.
- **Importance:** Confidence is essential for facing challenges, taking risks, and pursuing goals.

10. **Independence:**
- **Nature-Based Approach:** Engaging in solo activities like hiking promotes independence.
- **Importance:** Learning to be independent prepares teenagers for adulthood and builds a sense of responsibility.

11. **Mindfulness and Stress Management:**
- **Nature-Based Approach:** Spending time in nature promotes mindfulness and reduces stress.
- **Importance:** Managing stress is crucial for mental well-being, and mindfulness aids in focus and emotional regulation.

12. **Environmental Awareness:**
- **Nature-Based Activity:** Nature conservation projects, tree planting, or wildlife observation.

- **Importance:** Understanding and caring for the environment is vital for sustainable living.
- **Tips:** Educate teens on ecological systems, discuss environmental issues, and engage in activities that promote conservation.

Nature-based activity learning techniques provide a holistic approach to developing these life skills by combining experiential learning with the therapeutic benefits of being in nature. Encourage reflection and discussion after each activity to help teenagers connect their experiences to real-life situations.

"LoveVenture Getaway"

LoveVenture Getaway: An Inspirational Story

Story: "The Journey to Rekindle Love"

Characters:

- Amit: A hardworking IT professional, always engrossed in his job.
- Priya: A dedicated school teacher, feeling neglected due to Amit's busy schedule.

Setting:

The story takes place in the scenic foothills of the Himalayas, where Amit and Priya embark on a LoveVenture Getaway organized by LifeAdve.

The Strain: Amit and Priya had been married for five years, but lately, their relationship felt strained. Amit's demanding job left little time for them to connect, and Priya felt increasingly isolated. They argued more and laughed less, the spark in their relationship dimming with each passing day.

The Decision: Desperate to save their marriage, Priya came across a brochure for the LoveVenture Getaway. She convinced Amit to take a break from work and give their relationship a chance to heal. Reluctantly, he agreed, and they set off for the mountains, hoping to find the connection they had lost.

The Beginning: As they arrived at the picturesque retreat, they were welcomed by the serene beauty of nature. The first activity was a guided nature walk. The tranquillity of the forest and the fresh mountain air created an ideal setting for them to communicate openly. For the first time in months, Amit listened as Priya shared her feelings. They walked hand in hand, rediscovering the comfort of each other's presence.

Building Trust: The next day, they participated in team-building outdoor activities. Climbing a steep hill and navigating a challenging trail required them to trust each other implicitly. As they worked together to overcome obstacles, they began to rebuild the trust that had been eroded by their busy lives.

Quality Time: One evening, they enjoyed a starlit picnic. Lying on a blanket under the vast, twinkling sky, they reminisced about the early days of their relationship. The simplicity of the moment, away from the distractions of everyday life, allowed them to reconnect deeply.

Respect and Volunteering: During the getaway, Amit and Priya volunteered for an environmental project. Planting trees together symbolized nurturing their relationship. As they worked side by side, they developed a newfound respect for each other's dedication and values.

Emotional Intimacy: A couple's workshop focused on emotional intimacy. They shared their dreams, fears, and vulnerabilities, finding solace in each other's support. Amit realized how much he had taken Priya's presence for granted, and Priya appreciated Amit's efforts to reconnect.

Shared Goals: The couple set a joint fitness goal of hiking to a nearby peak. The journey was tough, but reaching the summit together was a testament to their shared determination. They celebrated their achievement, feeling a sense of unity and purpose.

Individual Growth: Recognizing the importance of personal development, Priya took up birdwatching, and Amit started photography. They encouraged each other's hobbies, understanding that personal growth would enhance their relationship.

Shared Interests: Discovering a mutual interest in photography, they spent hours capturing the beauty of nature. These shared activities created new bonds and happy memories.

Conflict Resolution: One afternoon, a disagreement arose. Instead of escalating, they took a nature walk to cool off. The calming effect of the forest helped them discuss their issues constructively, focusing on finding solutions rather than blaming each other.

Gratitude: Watching a breathtaking sunset together, they reflected on their journey. They expressed gratitude for each other's presence and the effort they both put into mending their relationship.

Rekindling Romance: The final night was a romantic campfire. The flickering flames and the starry sky created an intimate atmosphere. Amit and Priya shared heartfelt words and promises, rekindling the romance that had brought them together in the first place.

The Transformation: As their getaway came to an end, Amit and Priya felt rejuvenated. They returned home with a stronger bond, a deeper understanding of each other, and a treasure trove of shared memories. The LoveVenture Getaway had transformed their relationship, proving that with effort, communication, and the healing power of nature, love could indeed be rekindled.

Takeaways:

1. **Bond Strengthening:** Their emotional connection was renewed.

2. **Communication Enhancement:** Open and honest dialogues became a norm.

3. **Quality Time:** Prioritizing time together became a cherished practice.

4. **Adventure and Fun:** Shared adventures added excitement and joy.

5. **Conflict Resolution:** Constructive conflict resolution became their approach.

6. **Renewal of Romance:** The getaway reignited their passion.

7. **Memory Creation:** They created lasting, cherished memories.

8. **Novelty and Adventure:** New activities brought a sense of adventure.

9. **Relaxation and Stress Relief:** They learned to relax and rejuvenate together.

10. **Building Trust:** Overcoming challenges together strengthened their trust.

11. **Cultural Exposure:** They embraced new experiences and perspectives.

12. **Rekindling Romance:** Romantic settings reignited their love.

13. **Exploration of Shared Interests:** Shared hobbies fostered a sense of unity.

14. **Investment in the Relationship:** Their efforts showed a commitment to their partnership.

Conclusion: The Loveventure Getaway not only saved Amit and Priya's marriage but also made it stronger and more resilient. Their story stands as a testament to the power of nature, communication, and shared experiences in building and maintaining a healthy, loving relationship.

"LoveVenture Getaway"

What is "LoveVenture Getaway"?

"LoveVenture Getaway" is a well-organized, planned getaway, outing, journey designed for couples to spend quality time together and strengthen their relationship.

This involves activities such as workshops, adventure activities, simulated counseling sessions, or simply leisure and bonding experiences aimed at enhancing communication and connection between partners.

These excursions focus on shared experiences, communication, and quality time together.

The goal is to enhance the couple's connection, deepen their understanding of each other, and create lasting memories to strengthen their relationship.

Why?

Guaranteed Take Aways from "LoveVenture Getaway"

1. **Bond Strengthening:** Couples relationship excursions provide dedicated time for partners to bond and strengthen their emotional connection.

2. **Communication Enhancement:** The shared experiences during these excursions facilitate improved communication, fostering understanding and empathy.

3. **Quality Time:** Dedicated time away from routine allows couples to focus on each other, creating cherished memories and deepening their intimacy.

4. **Adventure and Fun:** Excursions offer opportunities for shared adventures and fun activities, injecting excitement and joy into the relationship.

5. **Conflict Resolution:** Time away from daily stressors provides a conducive environment for resolving conflicts and addressing relationship challenges.

6. **Renewal of Romance:** The change of scenery and break from routine rekindles romance, adding a spark to the relationship.

7. **Memory Creation:** Excursions create lasting memories, contributing to a shared history that can sustain a relationship through challenging times.

8. **Novelty and Adventure:** Trying new activities together adds excitement, injecting a sense of adventure into the relationship.

9. **Relaxation and Stress Relief:** Escaping from daily stresses allows couples to relax, rejuvenate, and relieve tension.

10. **Building Trust:** Shared experiences and overcoming challenges together contribute to building trust and a sense of partnership.

11. **Cultural Exposure:** Experiencing new environments and cultures broadens perspectives, encouraging personal growth and mutual understanding.

12. **Rekindling Romance:** Romantic settings and activities during excursions can reignite passion and romance in a relationship.

13. **Exploration of Shared Interests:** Excursions offer a chance to explore common interests, fostering a sense of shared identity and compatibility.

14. **Investment in the Relationship:** Actively participating in relationship excursions signifies a commitment to investing time and effort in the well-being of the partnership.

Building Healthy Couples' Relationship

Building healthy Couples' Relationship

Building and maintaining a healthy and progressive relationship involves a combination of factors and realizations. Nature-based activities can be a wonderful way to enhance these aspects of a relationship. Here are some important factors and tips:

1. **Communication:**
   - **Realization:** Effective communication is key to understanding each other's needs and concerns.
   - **Nature-Based Activity Technique:** Take a walk in a park or go hiking. The serene environment can encourage open and honest communication.
   - **Tips:** Practice active listening, express feelings clearly, and be open to discussing both positive and negative aspects.

2. **Trust:**
   - **Realization:** Trust is the foundation of a strong relationship.
   - **Nature-Based Activity Technique:** Participate in team-building outdoor activities. This can strengthen trust and cooperation.
   - **Tips:** Be reliable, honest, and consistent. Trust is built over time through consistent actions.

3. **Quality Time:**
   - **Realization:** Spending quality time together fosters a deeper connection.
   - **Nature-Based Activity Technique:** Plan a picnic, go camping, or stargazing. Nature-based activities provide a tranquil setting for quality time.
   - **Tips:** Be present in the moment, minimize distractions, and engage in activities you both enjoy.

4. **Respect:**
   - **Realization:** Mutual respect is crucial for a healthy relationship.
   - **Nature-Based Activity Technique:** Volunteer for environmental projects together. This can highlight the importance of respect for nature and each other.
   - **Tips:** Listen to each other's opinions, value differences, and avoid belittling or disrespectful behaviour.

5. **Emotional Intimacy:**
- **Realization:** Emotional intimacy fosters a deep connection and understanding between partners.
- **Tips:**

1. Share your fears, dreams, and vulnerabilities.

2. Be supportive during challenging times.

3. Show affection through words and actions.

6. **Shared Values & Goals:**
- **Realization:** Common aspirations contribute to a sense of purpose and unity.
- **Nature-Based Activity Technique:** Set joint fitness goals like hiking a certain trail or training for a charity run.
- **Tips:** Discuss and plan short-term and long-term goals together. Celebrate achievements as a team.

7. **Individual Growth & Independence:**
- **Realization:** Both partners should have room for personal development.
- **Nature-Based Activity Technique:** Encourage individual outdoor hobbies that allow personal growth, such as bird watching or photography.
- **Tips:** Support each other's aspirations, give space for personal pursuits, and celebrate individual achievements.

8. **Shared Hobbies and Interests:**
- **Realization:** Shared activities create bonds and shared memories.
- **Nature-based activity:** Explore new outdoor hobbies, such as birdwatching or photography.

- **Tip:** Find activities you both enjoy and make time for them regularly.

9. **Empathy:**
- **Realization:** Understanding and empathizing with each other's perspectives is crucial. Realize the impact of validating each other's emotions.
- **Nature-based Activity Technique:** Volunteer together for environmental or community projects, fostering a shared sense of empathy towards others.

10. **Intimacy:**
- **Realization:** Physical and emotional intimacy are essential for a thriving relationship.
- **Nature Technique:** Explore nature together, whether it's a beach vacation, stargazing, or a quiet evening in a secluded forest area, to create an intimate atmosphere.

11. **Adaptability:**
- **Realization:** Life is unpredictable, and adaptability is crucial for resilience.
- **Nature Technique:** Engage in activities that require flexibility, like spontaneous day trips or camping, to cultivate adaptability as a couple.

12. **Self-Care:**
- **Realization:** Taking care of oneself contributes to the overall well-being of the relationship.
- **Nature-Based Activity Technique:** Encourage each other to engage in outdoor solo activities for self-reflection and rejuvenation.

13. **Patience and Forgiveness:**
- **Realization:** Mistakes happen, and learning to forgive and be patient is essential.

- **Nature-Based Activity Technique:** Spend time in nature to reflect on challenges, fostering a sense of calm and patience.

14. Conflict Resolution:

- **Realization:** Disagreements are normal, and resolving them constructively is crucial.
- **Nature-Based Activity Technique:** Take a nature walk to cool off before discussing conflicts. Nature has a calming effect.
- **Tips:** Focus on the issue, not on blaming each other. Use "I" statements, compromise, and seek solutions together.

15. Gratitude:

- **Realization:** Expressing gratitude fosters a positive atmosphere.
- **Nature-Based Activity Technique:** Share a sunset or sunrise experience. Reflect on what you're grateful for in nature.
- **Tips:** Regularly express appreciation for each other. Small gestures can have a big impact.

Incorporating these factors and realizations through nature-based activities can provide a unique and enriching experience, fostering a deeper connection between partners. The natural environment often facilitates relaxation, open communication, and a sense of shared accomplishment, all of which contribute to a healthy and progressive relationship

"Grand Generational Bond"

The Tale of the Grand Generational Bond

In a small village in India, nestled among lush green hills and vibrant fields, lived a wise and loving grandmother named Meera and her curious, energetic grandson, Aarav. Meera had always believed in the power of family bonds and cherished every moment she spent with her grandson. Aarav, with his boundless energy and endless questions, brought a spark of joy into her life.

One day, Meera decided that it was time to create some lasting memories with Aarav. She planned a special trip, a "Grand Generational Bond" getaway, to a serene nature retreat. The retreat promised a variety of activities designed to strengthen the bond between grandparents and grandchildren. Excited about the adventure, Meera and Aarav packed their bags and set off on their journey.

As they arrived at the retreat, they were greeted by a beautiful landscape filled with tall trees, blooming flowers, and a clear, flowing river. Their adventure began with a nature walk. Walking hand in hand along the trail, Meera and Aarav marvelled at the beauty around them. Meera shared stories of her childhood, teaching Aarav about the plants and animals they encountered. Aarav listened with wide-eyed wonder, feeling a deeper connection to his grandmother and the natural world.

Next, they participated in a tree-planting activity. Meera explained the importance of taking care of the environment and the legacy of planting trees for future generations. Together, they planted a sapling, symbolizing their growing bond and shared responsibility for nature. Aarav felt a sense of pride and accomplishment, knowing that he was contributing to something lasting and meaningful.

In the evenings, they sat by the campfire, sharing stories and laughter. Meera recounted tales of her youth, imparting wisdom and life lessons. Aarav, inspired by his grandmother's stories, opened up about his dreams and fears. The campfire became a safe space for them to express their thoughts and emotions, strengthening their emotional bond.

One afternoon, they engaged in a nature-inspired art session. They collected leaves, rocks, and flowers to create beautiful art pieces. As they painted and crafted, Meera encouraged Aarav to use his imagination and explore his creativity. This activity not only sparked Aarav's artistic talents but also deepened their connection through shared creativity.

Throughout their stay, Meera and Aarav participated in various activities, from bird watching to nature journaling. Each activity brought them closer, teaching Aarav valuable life skills and instilling a sense of respect for nature and his heritage. Meera, in turn, felt a renewed sense of purpose and joy, knowing she was making a positive impact on Aarav's life.

On the last day of their getaway, Meera and Aarav took a moment to reflect on their experiences. They sat by the river, watching the sun set over the hills. Meera spoke about the importance of family traditions, values, and the love that binds generations together. Aarav, holding his grandmother's hand, promised to cherish these moments and carry forward the lessons he had learned.

As they returned home, both Meera and Aarav felt a profound sense of fulfilment. The "Grand Generational Bond" getaway had not only strengthened their relationship but had also created memories that would last a lifetime. They knew that no matter where life took them, the bond they shared would always be a source of love, wisdom, and strength.

Key Takeaways from the Story:

1. **Unconditional Love:** The getaway fostered a deep sense of unconditional love and support between Meera and Aarav.

2. **Wisdom and Guidance:** Meera shared valuable life lessons and wisdom through stories and activities.

3. **Family Traditions:** The experience emphasized the importance of preserving and passing down family traditions.

4. **Quality Time:** The activities provided opportunities for meaningful, quality time together.

5. **Mentorship:** Meera served as a mentor, guiding Aarav and offering a different perspective on life.

6. **Emotional Support:** The safe space created during the trip allowed for open emotional expression and support.

7. **Inter-Generational Learning:** Aarav learned new skills and gained insights from his grandmother.

8. **Role Modelling:** Meera's actions and teachings served as a role model for Aarav.

9. **Respect for Elders:** Aarav developed a greater respect and appreciation for his grandmother and elders in general.

10. **Legacy and Heritage:** The getaway reinforced the importance of cultural heritage and family legacy.

The "Grand Generational Bond" concept beautifully illustrates the powerful impact of inter-generational connections and the lasting benefits of spending quality time together in nature.

"Grand Generational Bond"

What is "Grand Generational Bond"?

"Grand Generational Bond" is a well-organized, planned getaway, outing, excursion designed for Grandparents and Grandchildren to spend quality time together and strengthen the bond between the generations.

Grandparent-grandchild relationships are often valued for the wisdom and experiences that grandparents can share with their grandchildren, and excursions or activities together can be a meaningful way to create lasting memories and foster a close connection.

This includes and involves activities such as workshops, adventure activities, cooking together, or simply leisure and bonding experiences or any other activity that allows for quality time and shared experiences between grandparents and grandchildren.

Why?

Guaranteed Take Aways from ""Grand Generational Bond""

1. **Unconditional Love:** Grandparents provide a unique source of unconditional love and support, fostering a secure emotional foundation for grandchildren.

2. **Wisdom and Guidance:** Grandparents share valuable life experiences, offering wisdom and guidance that contribute to the grandchildren's personal development.

3. **Family Traditions:** Grandparents play a crucial role in passing down family traditions, creating a sense of continuity and connection across generations.

4. **Quality Time:** Spending quality time together builds strong bonds. Grandparents can engage in activities that interest grandchildren, fostering a deeper connection.

5. **Mentorship:** Grandparents serve as mentors, providing a different perspective and life insights that can positively impact the grandchildren's decision-making.

6. **Emotional Support:** Grandparents offer a safe space for grandchildren to express themselves, providing emotional support and understanding during challenging times.

7. **Inter-Generational Learning:** Grandchildren benefit from learning new skills, hobbies, and cultural aspects from their grandparents, promoting inter-generational knowledge transfer.

8. **Role Modelling:** Grandparents serve as role models, imparting values, ethics, and principles that contribute to the grandchildren's moral development.

9. **Celebrating Milestones:** Grandparents play a crucial role in celebrating significant life events, reinforcing the importance of family bonds during joyous occasions.

10. **Respect for Elders:** Grandparent-grandchild relationships teach children the importance of respecting and appreciating the elderly, fostering empathy and compassion.

11. **Legacy and Heritage:** Grandparents help preserve and pass on cultural heritage, instilling a sense of pride and identity in grandchildren.

Road Map: "Grand Generational Bond"

Road Map: "Grand Generational Bond"

The grandparent-grandchild relationship is a unique and valuable bond that holds significance for various reasons. Planning and engaging in excursions together can further enhance this special connection. Here are some key points highlighting the importance of grandparent-grandchild relationships excursions:

1. **Emotional Bonding:**
- **Importance:** Grandparent-grandchild relationships foster emotional bonding, creating a sense of security and love.
- **Nature-based Activity:** Take nature walks together, explore parks, or have a picnic in a natural setting.
- **Tips:** Encourage open communication and share personal stories during these activities.

2. **Wisdom and Life Lessons:**
- **Importance:** Grandparents offer valuable life experiences and wisdom, providing guidance and perspective.
- **Nature-based Activity:** Plant a garden together, imparting the importance of growth and nurturing.
- **Tips:** Share stories of challenges and victories, emphasizing the lessons learned.

3. **Cultural and Family Heritage:**
- **Importance:** Grandparents play a vital role in passing down cultural traditions and family history.
- **Nature-based Activity:** Explore cultural events in nature, like outdoor festivals or historical sites.
- **Tips:** Share family stories, traditions, and recipes during outdoor gatherings.

4. **Health and Well-being:**
- **Importance:** Interactions with grandparents contribute to the overall well-being and happiness of grandchildren.
- **Nature-based Activity:** Engage in outdoor games, like frisbee or nature-inspired scavenger hunts.
- **Tips:** Encourage physical activity and healthy habits while enjoying the natural environment.

5. **Inter-generational Bond:**
- **Importance:** Building connections across generations strengthens the family unit and promotes a sense of belonging.
- **Nature-based Activity:** Camp together, fostering teamwork and inter-generational bonding.
- **Tips:** Create shared experiences that bridge generational gaps and create lasting memories.

6. **Moral and Ethical Values:**
- **Importance:** Grandparents can instil important moral and ethical values in their grandchildren.
- **Nature-based Activity:** Volunteer for environmental projects, teaching the value of giving back to the community.
- **Tips:** Discuss the importance of respect for nature and responsible environmental stewardship.

7. **Mental Stimulation:**
- **Importance:** Grandparents contribute to the cognitive development of grandchildren through storytelling and shared activities.
- **Nature-based Activity:** Bird watching or cloud gazing, encouraging observation and discussion.
- **Tips:** Engage in conversations that stimulate curiosity and critical thinking during outdoor activities.

8. **Respecting Differences:**
- **Importance:** Interacting with grandparents promotes acceptance and understanding of generational differences.
- **Nature-based Activity:** Attend cultural or natural events, fostering an appreciation for diversity.
- **Tips:** Encourage open-mindedness and celebrate differences through shared experiences.

9. **Support System:**
- **Importance:** Grandparents provide an additional layer of emotional support and a different perspective during challenging times.
- **Nature-based Activity:** Reflect on life while enjoying a scenic view or around a bonfire.
- **Tips:** Create a safe space for open communication and offer guidance when needed.

10. **Creating Lasting Memories:**
- **Importance:** Grandparent-grandchild relationships create cherished memories that last a lifetime.
- **Nature-based Activity:** Document experiences through nature journals or photo albums.
- **Tips:** Encourage storytelling and reminiscing during quiet moments in nature.

11. **Effective Communication and Active Listening:**
- **Activity:** Nature Walk and Talk
- **Importance:** Enhances bonding and encourages open communication.
- **Tips:** Choose a scenic trail and take turns sharing thoughts and experiences.

12. **Building Trust and Security:**
- **Nature Activity:** Bird Watching, Camping trip
- **Importance:** Encourages observation and patience. Creates a sense of security and trust through shared experiences
- **Tips:** Bring binoculars and a bird guidebook.

13. **Encouraging Creativity & Exploration:**
- **Nature Activity:** Nature Art (Leaf Pressing, Rock Painting)

- **Importance:** Inspires imagination and artistic expression. Stimulates curiosity and a love for discovery.
- **Tips:** Collect natural items for crafting.

14. Mentorship: Teaching Life Skills:

- **Nature Activity:** Camping Trip
- **Importance:** Develops survival skills and teamwork. Teaches responsibility, patience, and the joy of nurturing.
- **Tips:** Start with a backyard campout for beginners.

15. Fostering Respect for the Environment:

- **Nature Activity:** Tree Planting
- **Importance:** Instils a sense of responsibility for nature.
- **Tips:** Research native trees for your area.

16. Promoting Gratitude:

- **Activity:** Nature Journaling
- **Importance:** Cultivates mindfulness and appreciation for the environment.
- **Tips:** Take time during or after the activity to reflect on what they observed.

17. Balancing Screen Time:

- **Importance:** Provides an opportunity to disconnect and appreciate the beauty of the night sky.
- **Tips:** Learn about constellations together and discuss the importance of balancing screen time.

In conclusion, grandparent-grandchild relationships excursions are a meaningful investment in family ties, fostering connection, understanding, and love across generations. These shared experiences can leave a lasting impact on the individuals involved and contribute to the overall well-being of the family unit.

Early Adulthood Well-Being

Early Adulthood Well-being: An Inspirational Story

The Turning Point

Rahul, a 28-year-old software engineer in Bengaluru, felt the weight of the world on his shoulders. Balancing a demanding career, personal goals, and relationships left him feeling stressed and disconnected. He yearned for a change but didn't know where to start.

One evening, while scrolling through social media, Rahul stumbled upon a post about a nature retreat designed for young adults. The retreat promised career workshops, mindfulness practices, and opportunities to connect with others in a serene natural setting. Intrigued, Rahul signed up, hoping this experience might provide the clarity he desperately needed.

The Retreat Experience

The retreat was held in the lush Western Ghats, a few hours' drive from Bengaluru. Upon arrival, Rahul was greeted by the sound of birds and the sight of towering trees swaying in the breeze. The retreat organizers welcomed the group and outlined the activities planned for the weekend.

Career and Financial Stability: The first session involved outdoor networking events where participants shared their career goals while walking through forest trails. Rahul found himself brainstorming career ideas and receiving valuable advice from peers and mentors.

Identity Formation: One afternoon, the group embarked on solo hiking trips. Rahul used this time for self-reflection, journaling his thoughts as he sat by a serene waterfall. The solitude and beauty of nature helped him gain a clearer understanding of his strengths and aspirations.

Relationship Development: Evening campfires became a time for sharing stories and building friendships. Rahul bonded with a fellow participant, Priya, over their mutual love for hiking. They decided to plan regular nature outings together, strengthening their friendship.

Mental Health and Stress Management: Guided meditation sessions in the forest introduced Rahul to the concept of forest bathing. He felt his stress melt away as he immersed himself in the calming presence of nature. Outdoor yoga sessions further enhanced his mental well-being.

Intimacy and Connection: Rahul and Priya, now close friends, decided to go on a romantic hike during one of their outings. The serene environment allowed them to open up about their dreams and fears, deepening their emotional connection.

Health and Fitness: The retreat included outdoor sports and hiking activities. Rahul discovered a passion for trail running, which he continued after returning home, significantly improving his physical health and mood.

Personal Growth and Development: Workshops in natural settings focused on personal development and goal-setting. Rahul used this time to outline his career and personal growth plans, feeling more motivated and focused.

Time Management: Mindful walks through the forest taught Rahul the importance of balancing responsibilities and leisure. He began scheduling regular outdoor breaks to recharge and improve productivity.

Conflict Resolution: The retreat included sessions on effective communication and conflict resolution, held in serene natural settings. Rahul learned valuable skills for resolving conflicts constructively, which he later applied in his relationships.

Social Connection: Group nature outings and community gardening activities fostered a sense of belonging and social bonds. Rahul realized the importance of maintaining a supportive network beyond family.

Family Dynamics: Rahul invited his family for a weekend camping trip, using the opportunity to strengthen their bonds and facilitate open communication. The shared experience brought them closer together.

Spiritual Exploration: Meditation sessions in natural settings allowed Rahul to explore his personal beliefs and spirituality. He found peace and clarity, which he incorporated into his daily routine.

Technology Balance: The retreat enforced a digital detox, encouraging participants to disconnect from their devices. Rahul experienced the benefits of being present in the moment, which he continued by scheduling regular technology-free nature activities.

The Aftermath

Returning to Bengaluru, Rahul felt rejuvenated and transformed. He continued to incorporate nature-based activities into his routine, whether it was a morning run in the park, a weekend hike, or a solo retreat to the mountains.

The retreat had not only helped him navigate the challenges of early adulthood but also fostered a sense of well-being and balance. Rahul's relationships flourished, his career goals became clearer, and his mental and physical health improved. He realized that nature had provided him with the clarity and connection he had been seeking.

Rahul's journey is a testament to the transformative power of nature-based activities in enhancing well-being during early adulthood. By prioritizing time in nature, he discovered the tools needed to navigate life's challenges, build meaningful relationships, and achieve personal growth.

Key Takeaways:

- **Nature as a Catalyst:** Nature-based activities provide a powerful backdrop for personal and professional growth.

- **Self-Reflection:** Solitude in nature aids in understanding oneself, which is crucial for healthy relationships.

- **Connection and Communication:** Nature settings promote open communication, strengthening bonds.

- **Mental and Physical Health:** Regular nature-based activities improve overall well-being.

- **Balance:** Incorporating nature into daily routines helps balance responsibilities and leisure, enhancing productivity and focus.

By embracing nature, early adults can navigate the complexities of this life stage with greater clarity, resilience, and well-being.

Early Adulthood Well-being

1. **Early Adulthood (19 to 40 years):**
- **Importance:** Building intimate relationships becomes a focus. Friendships, family, and romantic relationships contribute to emotional support and personal growth.
- **Friendships and Professional Networks:** Building a social support system extends beyond family, with friendships and professional networks becoming key.

- **Challenges:** Balancing career, personal goals, and relationships. Navigating the transition to more mature, committed relationships.
- **Overcoming Challenges:** Prioritize communication and shared goals. Establish healthy boundaries. Invest time and effort in maintaining relationships.

Early adulthood is a crucial period of life marked by various challenges and concerns. Here are ten areas of concern related to early adulthood and relationship well-being, along with nature-based activity solutions, their importance, and tips:

1. **Career and Financial Stability:**
- **Concern:** Establishing a stable career and achieving financial independence.
- **Nature-Based Activity Solution:** Outdoor networking events, career retreats, or nature walks for brainstorming career goals.
- **Importance:** Nature activities can provide clarity and reduce stress, enhancing focus on career planning.
- **Tips:** Use nature as a backdrop for goal-setting and decision-making discussions.

2. **Identity Formation:**
- **Concern:** Developing a strong sense of self and identity.
- **Nature-based Solution:** Solo hiking or camping trips can provide time for self-reflection.
- **Importance:** Understanding oneself is crucial for healthy relationships.
- **Tips:** Try journaling or engaging in mindfulness practices in natural settings.

3. **Relationship Development:**
- **Concern:** Building and maintaining meaningful relationships.

- **Nature-Based Activity Solution:** Couples' retreats, hiking trips, or camping to strengthen bonds.
- **Importance:** Nature settings promote open communication and bonding, fostering healthy relationships.
- **Tips:** Plan regular nature outings to reconnect and share experiences.

4. **Mental Health and Stress Management:**
- **Concern:** Coping with stress and maintaining mental well-being.
- **Nature-Based Activity Solution:** Meditation in natural settings, forest bathing, or outdoor yoga.
- **Importance:** Nature has proven benefits for mental health, reducing stress and promoting relaxation.
- **Tips:** Incorporate nature-based activities into regular stress management routines.

5. **Intimacy and Connection:**
- **Concern:** Nurturing emotional and physical intimacy.
- **Nature-based Solution:** Romantic hikes or nature walks.
- **Importance:** Nature can create a serene environment for emotional connection.
- **Tips:** Plan nature-based activities to strengthen emotional bonds.

6. **Health and Fitness:**
- **Concern:** Maintaining a healthy lifestyle.
- **Nature-Based Activity Solution:** Outdoor sports, hiking, or running in natural environments.
- **Importance:** Nature-based exercises improve physical health and boost mood.
- **Tips:** Choose outdoor activities that align with personal fitness goals.

7. **Personal Growth and Development:**
- **Concern:** Continuous self-improvement and learning.
- **Nature-Based Activity Solution:** Solo nature retreats, workshops in natural settings.
- **Importance:** Nature facilitates reflection and personal growth.
- **Tips:** Use nature as a canvas for journaling and setting personal development goals.

8. **Time Management:**
- **Concern:** Juggling responsibilities and leisure.
- **Nature-Based Activity Solution:** Nature-inspired time management workshops, mindful walks.
- **Importance:** Nature helps in recharging and improving focus.
- **Tips:** Schedule outdoor breaks for enhanced productivity and well-being.

9. **Conflict Resolution:**
- **Concern:** Learning effective conflict resolution skills.
- **Nature-based Solution:** Couples' retreats in natural settings.
- **Importance:** Resolving conflicts constructively strengthens relationships.
- **Tips:** Utilize nature's calming influence for open and honest communication.

10. **Social Connection:**
- **Concern:** Balancing social life with other responsibilities.
- **Nature-Based Activity Solution:** Group nature outings, picnics, or community gardening.
- **Importance:** Nature activities foster community and social bonds.
- **Tips:** Combine socializing with outdoor activities to create a supportive network.

11. Family Dynamics:

- **Concern:** Navigating evolving roles within the family.

- **Nature-Based Activity Solution:** Family camping trips, nature-themed family gatherings.

- **Importance:** Nature activities strengthen family bonds and facilitate open communication.

- **Tips:** Use nature outings as opportunities for family discussions and quality time.

12. Spiritual Exploration:

- **Concern:** Exploring personal beliefs and spirituality.

- **Nature-Based Activity Solution:** Meditation in natural settings, spiritual retreats.

- **Importance:** Nature provides a serene backdrop for spiritual reflection.

- **Tips:** Engage in nature-based spiritual practices for a holistic experience.

13. Technology Balance:

- **Concern:** Managing screen time and digital overload.

- **Nature-Based Activity Solution:** Digital detox retreats, nature walks without devices.

- **Importance:** Nature helps in disconnecting and fostering in-person connections.

- **Tips:** Set designated times for technology-free nature activities.

Incorporating nature-based activities into various aspects of life during early adulthood can significantly contribute to overall well-being and personal development. These activities provide opportunities for reflection, connection, and a break from the demands of daily life. Remember, individual preferences vary, so it's important to choose activities that resonate personally.

Middle Adulthood Well-Being

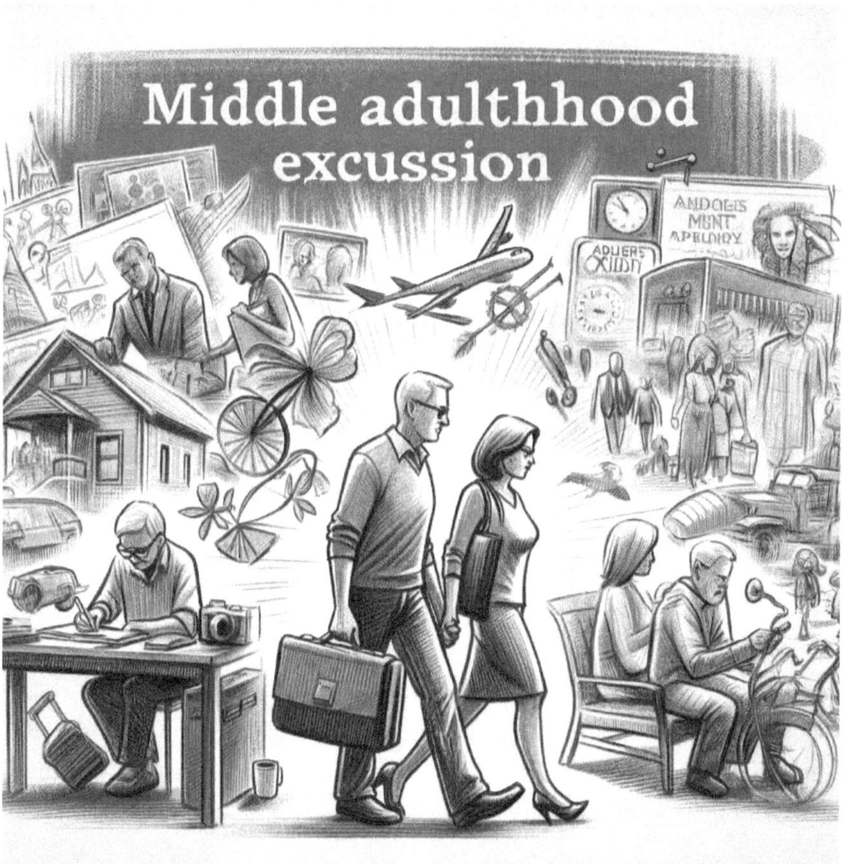

The Tale of Rekha: Embracing Middle Adulthood with Nature

Introduction

Rekha, a 45-year-old software engineer living in Bangalore, had always balanced her career, family, and personal life efficiently. However, as she approached middle adulthood, she began to experience the challenges typical of this life stage. Her children were growing up, her parents needed more care, and she felt increasingly dissatisfied with her job. Rekha decided to embrace these challenges with a new approach: integrating nature into her daily life.

Career and Job Satisfaction

Rekha often felt stagnant in her career, yearning for a sense of purpose. She attended an outdoor career counselling session held in a serene forest. The tranquil environment allowed her to reflect on her goals and aspirations. During a guided nature walk, she realized her passion for teaching and decided to explore opportunities in educational technology.

Tip: Regularly spend time in natural environments to enhance creativity and problem-solving skills.

Physical Health and Well-being

Rekha noticed that health issues were becoming more prominent. She started incorporating outdoor exercises like hiking and yoga into her routine. Every morning, she practiced yoga in her garden, finding it rejuvenating and calming.

Tip: Incorporate outdoor activities into your routine for a holistic approach to health.

Relationship Strain

With the stress of work and family responsibilities, Rekha's relationship with her husband, Raj, was strained. They decided to go on a couples' retreat in the hills. The retreat included activities like nature walks, campfire talks, and joint meditation sessions, which rekindled their bond.

Tip: Share outdoor activities to strengthen connections and build positive memories.

Parenting Challenges

Balancing parenting responsibilities was tough for Rekha. She organized family hikes and camping trips, which provided quality time together and strengthened their family ties. The shared experiences brought them closer, creating lasting memories.

Tip: Plan family outings to create lasting memories and strengthen family ties.

Financial Stress

The financial responsibilities of middle adulthood weighed heavily on Rekha. To cope, she planned budget-friendly camping trips with her family. They enjoyed these outings without extravagant expenses, focusing on the joy of being together in nature.

Tip: Enjoy nature without extravagant expenses, focusing on the experience rather than material costs.

Empty Nest Syndrome

When her eldest son left for college, Rekha felt a void. She and Raj took up bird watching and gardening, finding joy in these shared hobbies. These activities helped them reconnect as a couple and filled the emptiness they felt.

Tip: Plan outdoor activities that both partners enjoy to rekindle the relationship.

Cognitive Changes

Rekha was concerned about cognitive decline. She started engaging in memory-enhancing activities like nature walks and bird watching. These activities kept her mind sharp and provided a sense of peace.

Tip: Engage in activities like bird watching or nature walks to stimulate the mind.

Parenting Aging Parents

Caring for her aging parents was emotionally and physically demanding. Rekha encouraged her parents to join her on gentle nature walks. These outings provided relaxation and a mental break for both her and her parents.

Tip: Encourage the whole family to participate in outdoor activities to share the caregiving responsibilities.

Identity Crisis

Rekha experienced an identity crisis, questioning her purpose. She went on solo nature retreats, spending quiet time in the mountains. The peaceful setting allowed her to reconnect with her values and set new personal goals.

Tip: Spend quiet time in nature to reconnect with personal values and goals.

Social Isolation

Changes in social circles led Rekha to feel isolated. She joined a local hiking club, meeting like-minded individuals and forming new friendships. The social interactions in natural settings enhanced her well-being.

Tip: Participate in community nature events to meet like-minded individuals.

Technology Overload

Rekha realized that excessive reliance on technology was affecting her relationships. She implemented tech-free nature outings, such as weekend camping trips, fostering face-to-face interactions with her family.

Tip: Establish tech-free zones during nature activities to enhance connection.

Time Management

Balancing work, family, and personal time was challenging. Rekha scheduled regular nature breaks during her week, like short walks in the park during lunch breaks. These breaks rejuvenated her mind and improved her overall productivity.

Tip: Prioritize nature activities as essential for maintaining a healthy work-life balance.

Conclusion

Through these nature-based activities, Rekha navigated the challenges of middle adulthood with grace. She found clarity in her career, improved her health, strengthened her relationships, and rediscovered herself. Nature became her sanctuary, helping her embrace the complexities of this life stage and find fulfilment.

Key Takeaways

1. **Career Clarity:** Nature provides a peaceful setting for career reflection and decision-making.

2. **Health and Fitness:** Outdoor activities promote physical and mental well-being.

3. **Relationship Strengthening:** Nature fosters communication and bonding.

4. **Financial Relief:** Budget-friendly nature activities offer cost-effective stress relief.

5. **Cognitive Benefits:** Nature can help maintain cognitive health.

6. **Emotional Support:** Nature outings provide relaxation and stress relief for caregivers.

7. **Identity Exploration:** Quiet time in nature aids in personal introspection and goal-setting.

8. **Social Connections:** Community nature events help reduce social isolation.

9. **Reduced Screen Time:** Tech-free nature activities enhance face-to-face interactions.

10. **Balanced Life:** Regular nature breaks improve time management and productivity.

By integrating nature into various aspects of her life, Rekha not only overcame the challenges of middle adulthood but also found a path to greater well-being and happiness.

Middle Adulthood Well-being

Middle Adulthood (41 to 60 years):

- **Family and Work-Life Balance:** Nurturing relationships with a partner and children is essential, as is maintaining connections with friends and colleagues.

- **Parent-Adult Child Relationships:** Parents may experience evolving relationships with adult children, providing guidance and support as needed.

- **Challenges:** Juggling multiple responsibilities, potential midlife crises, and changes in family dynamics.

Overcoming Challenges: Prioritize time for relationships. Adapt to changes together. Seek support when needed. Here are areas of concern related to middle adulthood and relationship well-being, along with nature-based activity solutions, their importance, and tips:

1. **Career and Job Satisfaction:**
- **Concern:** Middle-aged individuals may face career stagnation or dissatisfaction.
- **Nature-Based Solution:** Outdoor career counselling sessions, nature retreats to reflect on career goals.
- **Importance:** Connecting with nature can provide clarity and a fresh perspective on career choices.
- **Tips:** Regularly spend time in natural environments to enhance creativity and problem-solving skills.

2. **Physical Health and Well-being:**
- **Concern:** Health issues may become more prominent in middle adulthood.
- **Nature-Based Solution:** Outdoor exercises such as hiking, jogging, or yoga in natural settings.
- **Importance:** Nature-based activities promote physical fitness and mental well-being.

- **Tips:** Incorporate outdoor activities into your routine for a holistic approach to health.

3. **Relationship Strain:**
- **Concern:** Marital or familial issues may arise during this life stage.
- **Nature-Based Solution:** Couples' retreats or family vacations in natural settings.
- **Importance:** Nature fosters communication and bonding, improving relationship dynamics.
- **Tips:** Share outdoor activities to strengthen connections and build positive memories.

4. **Parenting Challenges:**
- **Concern:** Balancing parenting responsibilities.
- **Nature-based Solution:** Family hikes, camping trips, or nature-based outings.
- **Importance:** Nature activities provide a platform for family bonding.
- **Tips:** Plan family outings to create lasting memories and strengthen family ties.

5. **Financial Stress:**
- **Concern:** Middle adulthood often involves increased financial responsibilities.
- **Nature-Based Solution:** Budget-friendly camping trips or nature-based hobbies.
- **Importance:** Nature activities can provide cost-effective stress relief.
- **Tips:** Enjoy nature without extravagant expenses, focusing on the experience rather than material costs.

6. **Empty Nest Syndrome:**
- **Concern:** Children leaving home may lead to feelings of emptiness.
- **Nature-Based Solution:** Joint outdoor hobbies or travel to reconnect as a couple.
- **Importance:** Nature facilitates shared experiences, helping couples rediscover their bond.
- **Tips:** Plan outdoor activities that both partners enjoy to rekindle the relationship.

7. **Cognitive Changes:**
- **Concern:** Cognitive decline may become noticeable in middle adulthood.
- **Nature-Based Solution:** Memory-enhancing activities in natural settings.
- **Importance:** Nature has cognitive benefits, potentially slowing down cognitive aging.
- **Tips:** Engage in activities like bird watching or nature walks to stimulate the mind.

8. **Parenting Aging Parents:**
- **Concern:** Caring for aging parents can be emotionally and physically demanding.
- **Nature-Based Solution:** Nature outings for relaxation and stress relief.
- **Importance:** Nature helps alleviate caregiver stress and provides a mental break.
- **Tips:** Encourage the whole family to participate in outdoor activities to share the caregiving responsibilities.

9. **Identity Crisis:**
- **Concern:** Middle adulthood may prompt a re-evaluation of personal identity.

- **Nature-Based Solution:** Solo nature retreats for self-reflection.
- **Importance:** Nature provides a peaceful setting for introspection and self-discovery.
- **Tips:** Spend quiet time in nature to reconnect with personal values and goals.

10. **Social Isolation:**
- **Concern:** Changes in social circles or friendships may lead to isolation.
- **Nature-Based Solution:** Join outdoor clubs or group activities.
- **Importance:** Nature-based social interactions enhance well-being and reduce isolation.
- **Tips:** Participate in community nature events to meet like-minded individuals.

11. **Technology Overload:**
- **Concern:** Excessive reliance on technology affecting relationships.
- **Nature-based Solution:** Implement tech-free nature outings or camping trips.
- **Importance:** Nature fosters face-to-face interactions and reduces screen time.
- **Tips:** Establish tech-free zones during nature activities to enhance connection.

12. **Time Management:**
- **Concern:** Balancing work, family, and personal time becomes challenging.
- **Nature-Based Solution:** Schedule regular nature breaks during the week.
- **Importance:** Nature rejuvenates the mind, improving overall productivity.

- **Tips:** Prioritize nature activities as essential for maintaining a healthy work-life balance.

In summary, incorporating nature-based activities into various aspects of life during middle adulthood can contribute to improved well-being, enhanced relationships, and effective coping with the challenges of this life stage. The key is to recognize the value of nature in promoting physical, mental, and emotional health, and to intentionally integrate it into one's lifestyle.

Late Adulthood Well-Being

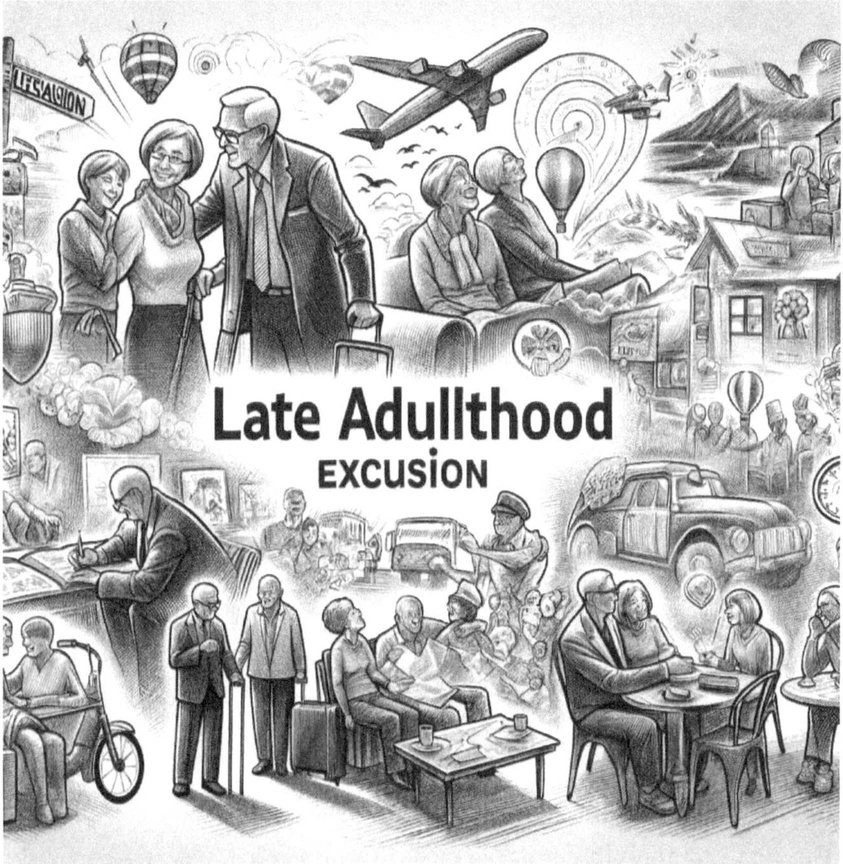

Late Adulthood Well-being: An Inspirational Story

Title: "The Healing Retreat"

Characters:

1. **Rajesh:** A retired teacher, struggling with physical health issues and the loss of his wife.

2. **Meera:** Rajesh's childhood friend, coping with cognitive decline and the isolation of living alone.

3. **Suresh:** A widowed neighbor dealing with the emotional strain of caregiving for his elderly mother.

4. **Lakshmi:** Rajesh's daughter, concerned about her father's well-being and encouraging him to join a nature-based retreat.

Setting:

An old-aged nature-based camping retreat in the lush countryside of Kerala, India.

Story:

Rajesh had always been an active man, but after retiring from his teaching job and losing his wife, he found himself sinking into a routine of inactivity and sorrow. His daughter, Lakshmi, had been persistently encouraging him to join a nature-based retreat designed for the elderly. Reluctantly, Rajesh agreed, and soon found himself on a bus heading to a serene campsite in Kerala.

Upon arrival, Rajesh was greeted by the retreat organizers and a group of other elderly participants, including Meera, his childhood friend, and Suresh, a neighbour he had lost touch with over the years. The camp was nestled among rolling hills, with a gentle river flowing nearby and a canopy of trees providing shade and tranquillity.

Day 1: Physical Health

The first morning, the group gathered for a gentle yoga session by the river. The instructor guided them through simple stretches and breathing exercises, focusing on improving mobility and flexibility. Rajesh, though initially hesitant, felt a renewed sense of vitality as he moved through the poses, the fresh air invigorating his spirit.

Tips: Encourage regular walks in nature, join senior fitness classes, or engage in activities like yoga for better balance and flexibility.

Day 2: Cognitive Health

In the afternoon, the participants were invited to join a bird-watching excursion. Armed with binoculars and a guidebook, they set out to identify the various birds inhabiting the area. Meera, who had been struggling with memory issues, found joy in this activity, as it stimulated her mind and brought back memories of her childhood days spent in nature.

Tips: Encourage participation in outdoor activities that engage the mind, like identifying different plants or animals.

Day 3: Social Isolation

As the days went by, the camp became a close-knit community. Group nature walks and community gardening sessions fostered social connections and camaraderie. Rajesh, Meera, and Suresh found solace in each other's company, sharing stories and laughter around the campfire each evening.

Tips: Join local clubs or community groups that focus on outdoor activities to foster social connections.

Day 4: Loss and Grief

One evening, the group participated in a memorial tree-planting ceremony. Each person planted a tree in memory of a loved one they had lost. Rajesh planted a sapling for his wife, feeling a profound sense of peace and connection as he did so. The act of nurturing the tree gave him a sense of purpose and comfort in his grief.

Tips: Encourage the individual to spend reflective time in nature to process grief and find peace.

Day 5: Loss of Independence

The camp featured accessible nature trails and adaptive gardening activities, ensuring that everyone, regardless of physical ability, could participate. Rajesh felt a renewed sense of independence as he navigated the trails and tended to the communal garden, his confidence growing with each passing day.

Tips: Provide resources for activities that accommodate physical abilities and promote autonomy.

Day 6: Role Transitions

Adjusting to retirement and new roles was a common theme among the participants. The camp offered opportunities for purposeful engagement, such as mentoring younger volunteers and sharing life stories. Rajesh found fulfilment in these activities, rediscovering a sense of identity and purpose.

Tips: Explore new hobbies, set realistic goals, and stay socially connected through outdoor pursuits.

Day 7: Financial Concerns

The retreat emphasized budget-friendly activities like picnics and hiking, proving that meaningful experiences didn't require significant financial investment. Rajesh and his friends enjoyed these simple pleasures, appreciating the beauty of nature without worrying about expenses.

Tips: Explore low-cost outdoor recreation options and community events.

Day 8: Caregiver Stress

Suresh, who had been a caregiver for his mother, found much-needed respite in the shared outdoor activities. He realized the importance of self-care and the need to seek support from others. The camp provided a space for him to relax and recharge, surrounded by nature.

Tips: Encourage caregivers to take breaks by engaging in nature-based activities together or seeking support groups.

Day 9: Adjusting to Retirement

Rajesh discovered new hobbies like birdwatching and photography during the retreat. These activities gave him a sense of purpose and joy, filling the void left by his retirement. He looked forward to continuing these hobbies after returning home.

Tips: Encourage exploration of new outdoor hobbies and volunteering in nature-related activities.

Day 10: Emotional Well-being

Daily nature walks and outdoor meditation sessions helped alleviate feelings of depression and anxiety. The participants found solace in the beauty of their surroundings; their spirits lifted by the serene environment. Rajesh felt his emotional well-being improve significantly, thanks to the regular outdoor activities.

Tips: Incorporate regular outdoor activities to improve mood and reduce stress.

Day 11: Relationship Strain

The retreat also focused on relationship well-being. Rajesh and his friends enjoyed romantic outdoor dinners and stargazing sessions, fostering deeper connections and intimacy. These experiences rekindled their appreciation for life's simple joys and the importance of maintaining emotional connections.

Tips: Explore new ways to connect intimately, such as enjoying nature together and maintaining open communication.

Day 12: Technology Adaptation

The camp offered nature-based technology workshops, teaching participants how to use apps for bird identification and navigation. Rajesh, initially sceptical about technology, found these sessions helpful and fun, bridging the gap between the natural and digital worlds.

Tips: Attend technology classes, seek help from younger family members, and explore nature-related apps and websites.

Day 13: Spiritual Well-being

Reflective walks and nature-based rituals helped participants explore their spiritual side. Rajesh found peace and a deeper sense of connection to the world around him, realizing the profound impact of nature on his spiritual well-being.

Tips: Encourage exploration of spiritual practices in natural settings to foster a sense of connection and purpose.

Conclusion:

As the retreat came to an end, Rajesh, Meera, and Suresh returned home with renewed spirits, a deeper appreciation for nature, and strengthened relationships. The healing power of the retreat had not only addressed their individual concerns but also fostered a sense of community and well-being that would last long after their time in Kerala.

Incorporating nature-based activities can be a valuable approach to address various concerns in late adulthood, promoting overall well-being and enhancing the quality of relationships. Tailoring these activities to individual preferences and abilities while considering the significance of maintaining a balanced and fulfilling life during this stage is crucial.

Key Takeaways:

1. Nature has a profound impact on physical, cognitive, and emotional well-being.

2. Social connections and community involvement are essential for mental health.

3. Purposeful engagement and new hobbies can provide a sense of identity and fulfillment.

4. Accessible nature activities can accommodate varying physical abilities and promote independence.

5. Simple, budget-friendly outdoor activities can bring joy and reduce financial stress.

6. By embracing these principles, individuals in late adulthood can find renewed vitality, deeper connections, and a greater sense of purpose and peace.

Late Adulthood Well-being

1. **Late Adulthood (61 years and beyond):**
- **Importance:** Social connections become crucial for mental health. Family relationships offer support and companionship.
- **Challenges:** Coping with loss, physical health decline, and potential isolation.

Overcoming Challenges: Stay socially active. Seek support from family and friends. Engage in community activities. Embrace changing dynamics with resilience.

Here are Important areas of concern in late adulthood, focusing on relationship well-being, along with nature-based activity solutions, their importance, and some tips:

1. **Physical Health:**
- **Concern:** Declining health and mobility.
- **Nature-Based Activity Solution:** Gentle exercises such as walking in parks or gardening.
- **Importance:** Maintaining physical health is crucial for overall well-being.
- **Tips:** Encourage regular walks in nature, join senior fitness classes, or engage in activities like yoga for better balance and flexibility.

2. **Cognitive Health:**
- **Concern:** Cognitive decline and memory issues.
- **Nature-Based Activity Solution:** Mindful activities like bird watching or nature meditation.
- **Importance:** Cognitive stimulation can help slow down cognitive decline.
- **Tips:** Encourage participation in outdoor activities that engage the mind, like identifying different plants or animals.

3. **Social Isolation:**
- **Concern:** Decreased social interactions.
- **Nature-Based Activity Solution:** Group nature walks or community gardening.
- **Importance:** Social connections contribute to mental and emotional well-being.
- **Tips:** Join local clubs or community groups that focus on outdoor activities to foster social connections.

4. **Loss and Grief:**
- **Concern:** Coping with the loss of friends or family.
- **Nature-Based Activity Solution:** Memorial tree planting or creating a garden in memory.
- **Importance:** Nature can provide solace and a sense of connection.
- **Tips:** Encourage the individual to spend reflective time in nature to process grief and find peace.

5. **Loss of Independence:**
- **Nature-Based Solution:** Accessible nature trails, nature-based exercise programs, or adaptive gardening.
- **Importance:** Maintaining independence through nature-based activities can boost self-esteem.
- **Tips:** Provide resources for activities that accommodate physical abilities and promote autonomy.

6. **Role Transitions:**
- **Concern:** Adjusting to retirement and changing roles.
- **Nature-based Solution:** Engaging in purposeful outdoor activities, like mentoring or volunteering.
- **Importance:** Maintains a sense of purpose, identity, and community involvement.

- **Tips:** Explore new hobbies, set realistic goals, and stay socially connected through outdoor pursuits.

7. **Financial Concerns:**
- **Concern:** Economic insecurity and financial stress.
- **Nature-Based Activity Solution:** Budget-friendly outdoor activities like picnics or hiking.
- **Importance:** Financial stability contributes to mental and emotional well-being.
- **Tips:** Explore low-cost outdoor recreation options and community events.

8. **Caregiver Stress:**
- **Concern:** Balancing the role of caregiver.
- **Nature-Based Activity Solution:** Shared outdoor activities with the person being cared for.
- **Importance:** Caregivers need respite and self-care for their well-being.
- **Tips:** Encourage caregivers to take breaks by engaging in nature-based activities together or seeking support groups.

9. **Adjusting to Retirement:**
- **Concern:** Loss of work-related identity and routine.
- **Nature-Based Activity Solution:** Pursuing hobbies like birdwatching or photography.
- **Importance:** Finding purpose and meaning in retirement is essential.
- **Tips:** Encourage exploration of new outdoor hobbies and volunteering in nature-related activities.

10. **Emotional Well-being:**
- **Concern:** Depression, anxiety, or loneliness.

- **Nature-Based Activity Solution:** Nature walks, outdoor meditation, or art in nature.
- **Importance:** Nature has proven benefits for mental health.
- **Tips:** Incorporate regular outdoor activities to improve mood and reduce stress.

11. **Relationship Strain:**
- **Concern:** Changes in sexual intimacy and communication.
- **Nature-Based Activity Solution:** Romantic outdoor dinners or stargazing.
- **Importance:** Intimacy contributes to emotional connection and relationship satisfaction.
- **Tips:** Explore new ways to connect intimately, such as enjoying nature together and maintaining open communication.

12. **Technology Adaptation:**
- **Concern:** Difficulty adapting to technology for communication and information.
- **Nature-based Solution:** Nature-based technology workshops or outdoor tech activities.
- **Importance:** Facilitates communication, access to information, and tech literacy.
- **Tips:** Attend technology classes, seek help from younger family members, and explore nature-related apps and websites.

13. **Spiritual Well-being:**
- **Concern:** Questions about life purpose and existential concerns.
- **Nature-Based Activity Solution:** Nature-based rituals or reflective walks.
- **Importance:** Finding spiritual meaning can enhance overall well-being.

- **Tips:** Encourage exploration of spiritual practices in natural settings to foster a sense of connection and purpose.

In summary, incorporating nature-based activities can be a valuable approach to address various concerns in late adulthood, promoting overall well-being and enhancing the quality of relationships. It's important to tailor these activities to individual preferences and abilities while considering the significance of maintaining a balanced and fulfilling life during this stage.

Feedback Form

We value your feedback! Please take a few moments to share your thoughts and experiences with the book.

1. Overall Rating

On a scale of 1 to 5, how would you rate the book?

[ ] 1 – Poor   [ ] 2 – Fair   [ ] 3 – Good   [ ] 4 - Very Good   [ ] 5 - Excellent

2. Content and Relevance

Did the content of the book meet your expectations?

[ ] Yes   [ ] No   If no, please explain: ___

3. Most Impactful Section

Which section or chapter of the book did you find most impactful?

4. Practical Application

How likely are you to apply the activities and lessons from the book in your daily life? [ ] Very Likely [ ] Likely   [ ] Neutral   [ ] Unlikely   [ ] Very Unlikely

5. Suggestions for Improvement

Do you have any suggestions for improving the book?

6. Additional Comments

Please share any additional comments or thoughts:

7. Interest in Further Resources

Would you be interested in accessing more resources, workshops, or programs related to the book's themes?   [ ] Yes   [ ] No

8. Contact Information (Optional)

If you'd like to receive updates, newsletters, or information on related workshops, please provide your contact details:

Name:___

Email:___

Domain: lifeadve.online

Note: For further information, practical application of the concepts, and access to additional resources, please scan the QR code below to download our app or visit our website www.lifeadve.com.

www.ingramcontent.com/pod-product-compliance
Lightning Source LLC
LaVergne TN
LVHW091703070526
838199LV00050B/2263